Keeping the Faith

passages ○ proverbs ○ parables

To Marcy,

May you always hold to the faith you need!

Copyright © 2008 Ronnie McBrayer

ISBN 978-1-60145-611-3

All rights reserved. No part of this publication may be reproduced, stored in a retrieval system, or transmitted in any form or by any means, electronic, mechanical, recording or otherwise, without the prior written permission of the author.

Printed in the United States of America.

A Leaving Salem Book Project (www.LeavingSalem.net)
2008

Cover Art by Michael and Laura Granberry

Keeping the Faith

passages ◦ proverbs ◦ parables

Ronnie McBrayer

From The Readers Of *Keeping The Faith*

"Ronnie, God has given you an incredible gift to bring many people closer to Him. I am one of those people and I thank you." – Terri

"I grew up in an environment like yours. It has made understanding and accepting grace very difficult at times. *Keeping the Faith* is refreshing." – William

"Is it just me, or is that guy Ronnie McBrayer always on target. He is the best writer your paper has." – Robert

"I have had an edge of discontent for years. Thanks for reinforcing it. I think." – Jimmy

"You are wrong about the Rapture, among other things. I fear you will be one of the many who are left behind." – Charles

"You're writing is superb! You have found your true calling." – Pat

"I'm not sure why I'm writing, but I feel I must tell you that God has used your words to bring healing to my life. Thank you." – Karli

"I can hardly wait to read *Keeping the Faith* each week. Thank you, thank you, thank you!" – Van

"Today I read your article in the *Sun*. I always do. Your words have sustained me many times in recent years." – Anne

"I must say that I look forward to reading your column and always finish the article with a true, real life message. May God keep your thoughts and words following His direction." – Tess

"I don't think you believe in hell. One day you will." – Tammy

"I enjoyed your latest article on faith and fun. I find this holy stuffiness rather interesting…and abundant." – Jessica

"I hope you realize the influence you have on others; the way you graciously challenge people's thinking. Keep it up, Ronnie." – Doug

"We've been taking a break from church for almost a year, avoiding the bull shit. It is rare to find people of like mind and heart in our life's journey, so thank you for writing." – Bala

"I really, really enjoy your weekly column. Please keep me in your prayers." – Mark

"All I can say is WOW! Your meanderings speak to a part of my heart that God has been stirring." – Brenda

"I always clip your articles from the paper and mail them to my daughter. Thank you!" – Faye

"Believers like you, if I can even call you one, are what is wrong with the church and this country. I will pray for you." – Stephen

"I appreciate the things you have to say, and to be honest, I was surprised that there was anyone saying it." – Bill

"I read your article this morning, as I do every Saturday. You always put it wonderfully into words." – Sharon

"Just so you know, my mother cut this week's *Keeping the Faith* out of the *Sun*, put it on her refrigerator, and mailed copies to all her children." – Michael

"Jesus, Jesus, Jesus – Is that all you've got to say?" – Leonard

"Thank you. It's great to know that there are other people in the same boat as me...or should I say, "out of the boat?" – Sandy

"I know a lot of people who consider your column part of their must-reading for the week. They find inspiration and faith in your words." – Gwen

"If people listen to you, there wouldn't be very many real churches left. Do you want that on your conscience?" – Nancy

"I should mention that I am an atheist and do not share your specific beliefs. But your writings strike a tone of simplicity and hope that I need. I read your column every week." – Kimberly

For Phil and Lee Ann Amico

If I get it all down on paper, it's no longer inside of me,
Threatening the life it belongs to;
And I feel like I'm naked in front of the crowd
Cause these words are my diary, screaming out loud
And I know that you'll use them, however you want to.

– Anna Nalick

Table of Contents

Preface xi

PASSAGES 1
   Of Fog And Faith 3
   I Haven't Moved 6
   "Judy Burgers" And Hope 9
   I Wonder About Your Wonder Bread 12
   Baseball And Baptists 15
   Fences 18
   Promises Kept 21
   The Monastery Master Mix 24
   Get Out Of The Way 27
   Old Man River 30
   Holiday Heresy 33
   WHY? 36
   One Hell Of A Sermon 39
   Summer 42
   Homesick 45
   Can You Hear Me Now? 48
   For Charles 51
   Is There Any Hope? 55
   The Will And Won't Of God 58
   Fools And Drunks 61

PROVERBS 65
   Some Assembly Required 67
   What Do I Turn Now? 70
   Strike Three, Surdykowski, Strike Three 73
   Warning: This Is Controversial 77
   The Gospel According To Rwanda 80
   McDonaldization 83
   Sprinkles 86
   My Jesus Is Better Than Your Jesus 89

Which Path To Peace?...92
God @#%!...95
Babushka...98
Have A Coke And A Smile!..101
The Hazards of Gallbladders And Glove Boxes....................104
Crashing Computers, Crashing Faith......................................107
Up The Hill Again…And Again…And Again…....................110
Ite Missa Est..113
Unwrapped...116
Low Food Or No Food..119
Of Jackrabbits And Jethro...122
Bad Juju...125

PARABLES 129
Catch The Wave...131
He Who Must Not Be Named...134
Jump..138
Color Blind..141
Spinning My Wheels...144
Sancta Ignorantia..147
If Only Speedy Had Been More…Speedy.............................150
Red, Red Wine..153
This Is Just Like Church...156
Please Talk To Me!...159
Take A Mulligan...162
This Is Going To Be Good..165
The Wheels On The Bus...168
All You Can Do Is All You Can Do.......................................171
Ode To Barley...174
The Preacher 177
My Last $5 180
Who Will Roll Away The Stone?...183
Blue Bomber...186
God Is In The Goulash..189

About The Author...193

Preface

In the summer of 2006 I began writing a faith column for my local newspaper, a Freedom Communications Publication called the *Walton Sun* (**www.waltonsun.com**). Publisher Rick Thomason and Editor Gwen Break enthusiastically supported me and "Keeping the Faith" was born. At the time I had a book deal or two on the line, but was a novice writer, and I still am. But Rick and Gwen rolled the dice, and for that I am grateful.

"Keeping the Faith" won the 2006 Florida Press Association Award in Religion, (which is curious, as I'm harder on the church and religion than most), and is now read by thousands of people every week and who knows how many more through internet syndication at my personal website, **www.leavingsalem.net**.

This collection contains sixty of my readers' favorite articles over the last couple of years, and I hope you find them as meaningful as the original readers did. As these articles were first printed in the *Walton Sun*, so they appear here, with little editing.

So enjoy, my friends. Think, converse, and laugh. Be inspired, be challenged, and surprised. And drop me a line to let me know if these flimsy words find a home in your heart.

I hope this book will live up to its name for you and your life.

Ronnie McBrayer
October 2008

PASSAGES

Of Fog And Faith

A parishioner walked up to me after a recent Sunday meeting and gushed, "I wish I had half as much faith as you!" I laughed in his face.

Quickly I tried to explain that while I may serve as a pastor my faith is as rickety as doubting Thomas'. Like so many, I find it challenging to maintain any level of real trust in God, in the church, or in my own decision to follow Christ. Living in this insane asylum we call planet Earth is enough to grind the truest believer into the dust, no?

So how do we do it? How do we keep the faith when it is sometimes so hard to believe? There is so much we cannot be certain of; so few things we actually control; so little that can be proven. Is following Christ and believing in God nothing more than Pascal's wager – a bet that the life we have chosen is true? Well, yes.

Largely, faith is not a foolish, misplaced emotion. It is a decision. We believe because we have chosen to believe. We will never understand all there is about Christian spirituality, about following Jesus, or how faith is best expressed in the world. But we do not have to understand it all. For in believing, we begin the life-long, eternity-long journey toward understanding. As we seize with faith the day that is before us, God opens our eyes to His reality, to see what actually is.

Often we get caught with the cart in front of the horse. We want to understand, first. We want certainty. We want iron-clad answers and assurances. Those things may come to you – they may not. But the way of Christ does not begin with confidence and move toward faith. It begins with faith and moves toward confidence (sometimes, but not always).

A few years ago I returned to Atlanta, Georgia, from Washington DC. It was a cold, stormy night. My flight had escaped Reagan National Airport just before a blizzard shut down the Eastern seaboard. But escape from the nation's capitol was not an escape from trepidation. The homeward flight was swallowed with clouds as thick as bricks. The cloud cover was so dense that as we entered our holding pattern over Atlanta, I could not even see the lights below – not a single light, not a single landmark.

The seatbelt was so tight around my waist that my kidneys were screaming "uncle." As we circled and circled, lurched and jerked, accelerated and dropped, I dug my fingernails deeper and deeper into the arm rests. Then, without word or warning, I felt the hardened thud of striking the runway. Safe and sound we coasted to the terminal.

Incredibly the pilot had landed the plane, not only in the dead of night, but in zero visibility. As I disembarked from the plane the pilot was standing at the door – sort of like the preacher at the end of Sunday worship – shaking hands, thanking us for our patronage and wishing us a fine evening. I stopped, and pointing out the window asked him, "How did you land this plane in that?"

He answered, "It was no sweat. I just trust the instruments."

If this pilot had tried to feel his way toward Atlanta, using his senses for some glimpse of certainly, we would have never made it home. We would have attempted a landing on Interstate 85 somewhere, or worse, have missed the city completely. To fail to trust the instruments – pointing us along on the journey – would have been a disaster.

Most times we can't see what waits for us on our way home. The clouds are too thick; the view too obscured. We can't even see where our next footstep will land. But in the absence of certainty, we reach forward in faith. God has placed the occasional marker as he speaks to us through his instruments – the Scriptures, in prayer, through the wisdom of those around us – and we trust those instruments to point us in the right direction.

The pilot who answered me so confidently as I left the plane that evening was skilled at hiding his fear. But he could not hide the circles of sweat that bled through the underarms of his coat. Still, sweating bullets or not, his trust in the instruments had gotten us home.

It always will.

I Haven't Moved

An old man and an old woman who had been married for many years were driving to church one Sunday morning. They fell in behind another car being driven by a young man. He was of college age or younger. Sitting beside the young man was a young woman, obviously his girlfriend. In fact, she was sitting so close to him that a credit card could not have been slipped between them. She was almost sitting in his lap, her head resting on his shoulder.

The old woman grew nostalgic. She began to think of her and her husband's younger years when they were so in love with each other. They used to drive up and down the strip of their home town every Friday night just like the young couple now in front of them.

She turned to her husband sitting behind the steering wheel on the other side of the front seat. Accusingly, almost bitterly, she said, "Look at them. Look at how they love each other. Why don't we drive through town like that any more? Why don't we sit that close together like we used to?"

She was met with silence. Her husband said not a word. After a few minutes the old man looked over at his wife and said, "I haven't moved."

God sometimes seems so far away, doesn't he? At times we think he's playing hide-and-seek at worst or peek-a-boo at best. But he's not. He's there, right where he has always been. He hasn't moved.

The Bible tells us to "Draw near to God." Draw near the immovable, always present, always graceful God. And when we do that, he will draw near to us. Scoot across the seat. Take a step toward him – even a halting, feeble step – and he will come running to you.

Most Christians live under the idea that God secretly dislikes us. He's the cosmic traffic cop maintaining the mother of all speed traps, itching to write a ticket and meet his quota of the condemned. There he is in our rearview mirror. Our palms sweat. Our body tightens. We drive through life terrified that the smirking, mirror-lensed God is about to turn on the blue lights. Surely he's out to get us.

Yet, God is not after you. What do you think the cross was all about? Why was God hanging on that piece of wood? The cross means that sin's back has been broken, not we his children.. We have been set free from fear and dread, and given a worth that exceeds the wealth and creation of the world. The cross, if it means anything at all, means we are welcomed into God's loving arms.

My children sometimes drive me absolutely insane. I'm talking bonkers; Dr. Jekyll to Mr. Hyde; Bruce Banner to the Incredible Hulk kind of insane. I lose my cool. I rant and rave. I lose patience; all those things that parents regrettably do. I want my children to obey me. I want them to respect me and honor me as their father.

But, in spite of my fits of frustration, I do not want my children to be afraid of me. I don't want them to feel that they must keep their distance, or that I'm out to get them.

Even when they are on my do-do list, I want them to come in, sit in my lap and talk to me. I want them to feel welcome. And they are. Why? Because they are my children. I want them to draw near, even more so when things are not going as good as they should be. How much more with our heavenly father?

Draw near to God. Through prayer and stillness, crawl into his lap and listen. Cry out with your frustrations, your fears, and your anger. He can take it. He welcomes it. Get quiet long enough to experience his embrace, and his love. Look at that cross and realize that he has given you the greatest thing he ever could, and he loves you with a love that is so high, so long, so deep and so wide that all of eternity will not be enough time to comprehend it.

The traffic cop God should be avoided, but not the God revealed to us in Jesus the Christ. Draw near to God and he will draw near to you.

"Judy Burgers" And Hope

The wife of my best friend has been diagnosed with cancer. Her name is Robin. She is thirty-seven-years old, the mother of four beautiful school-aged children, and one of the most undeserving cancer patients in the history of the world. But Clint Eastwood, philosophical about life, said "Deserves got nothing to do with it." I guess not.

Five years ago Robin beat back breast cancer with a double mastectomy, radiation and chemotherapy. When her tumor count, just weeks ago, was found to be suddenly high she returned to her oncologist to find cancer cells in her vertebrae, her lung, and two lymph nodes behind her sternum.

Her husband and I have been friends since we were fifteen-years-old. We sat side-by-side on the night of our high school graduation and took our senior trip together. I stood up for him at his wedding. I sat in on his ordination service. I held all his new-born babies and he mine. When we were living closer together, some fifty miles apart, we would meet at this little drug store café in Fairmount, Georgia, and have a "Judy Burger." I don't know who Judy is but she's makes a great burger, especially when it's covered with her chili.

There we would discuss everything from dispensationalism and John Calvin to the Southern Baptist Convention and what deacons in our church we would like to see swallowed up by the earth. We didn't always see eye to eye. We still don't. But he is the best friend I have had over more than twenty years, and here we are at this most difficult time in his life.

As different as we are, theologically and otherwise, we are now both asking the same questions: Why? Why them? Why Robin? Why this path for those so young, so committed to doing God's work, to those with young children, to those so undeserving? And as different as we are, theologically and otherwise, we still come to the same conclusion: Cancer in Robin's body – in your or my body – does nothing to change the fact that God still reigns over his creation.

Have we forgotten that we live in a fallen, fractured world? Have we forgotten that every "man born of woman has but a few days and they are full of trouble?" Have we forgotten that our years pass as quickly as a mist in the morning?

All of creation – cancerous bodies, broken hearted-widows, orphaned children, earthquake-ravaged China, war-torn Iraq, those of us with more questions than answers – we all long for God's new creation and redemption to come. Remember, this is not all there is. This is not even a fraction of all that is.

We live on the tip of an iceberg with the vastness of all God is and has planned for our futures lying somewhere beneath the surface. This life is the birth canal for that life to come. The sufferings of this present world are contractions pushing us forward into the future. This is a fallen, traumatized, unjust, unfair, brutal world begging for salvation. Those are the rules of engagement. These are the laws that govern this jungle.

So I have quit asking why "bad things happen to good people," for this is a bad world. The only real question I have left is "God, what are you waiting for?" But wait we must, in faith, knowing that God will one day return to the creation he has made, though he is never far away, to set things right, to exercise justice and mercy, and the knowledge of the Lord will fill the earth like the waters cover the sea.

This is our hope: That at the end of our lives, even at the end of this world, it will not be the end at all. Through the resurrection of our bodies and the recreation of heaven and earth, it will be the beginning.

Though we live in the tension and injustice of today, on blessed occasion, like lightning striking out of the East, a glimpse of the future comes rushing to us. Thankfully, the Divine wind blows just right and the clouds that darken this life's mirror clear, and we can see the light on the other side.

So be encouraged my friends. Keep the faith. Say your prayers and press on. What we suffer now is nothing compared to the wonder that will be revealed.

Addendum: At the time of this printing Robin is doing well with her husband Chad, and their four children.

I Wonder About Your Wonder Bread

"If there was one last loaf of bread in this town it would be mine."

I swear that's what he said. "He" being a rather pretentious member of the clergy, stating how God would take care of him should the world come unhinged tomorrow.

"Everyone else may starve to death, but I won't. God has promised me that I will never go without," he trumpeted.

Astonishment flashed across my face like racing neon lights. I didn't even try to mask it. In fact, I took a small step backwards and waited for the fire to fall.

But this strutting preacher quickly defended his statement by quoting Psalm 37:25 – "I have never seen the godly abandoned or their children begging for bread." See, this fine man considered himself godly. Righteous. Virtuous. Favored by God. Thus, no harm would ever befall him or his family. They lived the divinely-charmed life with no worries about the future for God had written him a blank check. "I've got God's promise," he kept saying.

The spiritual mathematics of this kind of self-confidence looks like this: "I am godly = I will always have what I need and never go without." For him the corollary is also true: "You are not very godly = You will not always have what you need, and you may go without."

Keeping the Faith

To hear him tell it, those who please God always land on top of the heap. Their cupboards are always full, their gas tanks never empty, their table always running over, and their checks never bounce. The reward for righteous living is a full belly.

But what about the godly Christians of yesteryear who did literally starve to death? Women like missionary Lottie Moon who gave her food away to the Chinese she served, only to die of malnutrition herself? There is St. Lucian of Rome, and countless others like him, who was starved to death in a prison cell because he would not renounce Christ? Or the 2.5 million souls facing starvation in Sudan, now as you read these words, many of whom are Christians? And going without bread is not the only disaster to fall upon the faithful. Christians in China suffer daily under the ruthlessness of that regime. Believers living in radicalized Islamic countries are persecuted at all levels of society. Faithful followers of Christ, even here in the West, daily bear the economic and social consequences of living out their faith.

Is there something wrong with the faith of these people who meet trouble? Has suffering come upon them because they are unrighteous? Are they bad Christians? Is this the explanation for their misery? See, I don't think this little mantra will hold up for long; this idea that righteous living always leads to the good life. Countless numbers of good and godly people have suffered, have gone without, have been tortured, have been chained in prison, and have died by stoning, firing squad, holocaust, and worse.

Why? Because they possessed an inferior faith, a faith not big or strong enough to get them out of trouble? No. They suffered because of their good and great faith, not an absence of it. The writer of the book of Hebrews concludes that those who suffer this way are "too good for this world...and earn a good reputation because of their faith."

Their stomachs didn't growl because their faith was defective. On the contrary, they suffered because of their virtue. They met painful ends, not because God was against them, but because God was for them. These heroes of faith weren't standing behind a pulpit, in the midst of chaotic times, bragging about how the last bread truck in town was going to make a special delivery to their home, sent there by God himself. No, they led a life of faith, a life lived in scorn of the consequences, taking virtue as reward enough.

After leaving the man who had called dibs on the last loaf of Wonder Bread in town, I was left to wonder myself. "What happens to this kind of faith when the promised bread truck doesn't arrive; when the pantry is found to be empty; when the last check bounces?"

I imagine a chink in this armor of belief makes for one hell of a crisis of faith. And it should. Faith that leads to arrogance isn't faith at all.

Baseball And Baptists

Major League Baseball and the burgeoning mega-church church down the street from my house: I have developed a suspicion of both of these, and for many of the same reasons. Don't get me wrong. I love baseball, and I love the church. But something is not quite right. Let me explain.

After the baseball players strike of the mid-1990s I fell off the wagon. Hard. The more recent scandal involving performance enhancing drugs and the obscene amounts of money paid to mere mortals for throwing and striking a rawhide ball have done nothing to reclaim my confidence. And have you taken your kids to a game lately? $25 to park, $75 for tickets, $60 for sodas and snacks. And forget the souvenirs; I haven't got that kind of cash.

What makes all this so difficult to take is the fact that some of my fondest memories hover around professional baseball. I'm not old, but old enough to remember sitting in the now demolished Atlanta-Fulton County Stadium trying to snag foul balls off the bats of Brett Butler, Dale Murphy, and Bob Horner: All for $3 at the turnstile. And I was in the stands the afternoon the Atlanta Braves won the National League pennant, completing their worst to first season of 1991. But I can count on one hand how many times I've been back since.

Some of my fondest memories were also made at church. In the little "church in the wildwood" of my most formative years, the pew bottoms were made of old wooden slats that creaked and groaned during the service, pinching this little boy's behind and picking holes in my mother's panty hose. The church's water fountain was a natural spring a hundred yards down a path behind the sanctuary. A visit to the toilet was a similar trek.

On hot August nights I can still recall the fiery summer revivals in that old house of worship – fiery in preaching and temperature – as I struggled to understand all that was going on (between explorations for Double Mint and Juicy Fruit gum in my grandmother's purse, of course).

Was this church "better" than what I experienced later as an adult? Probably not. Was it simpler, more sincere? Probably so.

Major League Baseball and much of the church in America have arrived at the same place. Both are more driven by market and commercial forces than by a true sense of what they are. They have largely been taken captive by the consumer, by self-indulgence, and vanity. We are all the worse for it.

My children thrill me on the baseball diamond every spring, even when they are picking flowers in the outfield or still putting their mitt on the wrong hand. There is an enjoyment, a purity in their play, that while unprofessional, is much more real than anything happening at the ball parks of big business. This is my same longing for the church. For I still love it and pray that it becomes less captive to American commercialism, more true to itself, more authentic.

Keeping the Faith

Terence Mann, James Earl Jones' character in *Field of Dreams*, may have captured the sentiment best. Speaking of those with this same longing, and standing in that miraculous cornfield turned baseball diamond, he says to Kevin Costner's character Ray Kinsella:

"They'll walk out to the bleachers; sit in shirtsleeves on a perfect afternoon. They'll find they have reserved seats somewhere along one of the baselines, where they sat when they were children and cheered their heroes. And they'll watch the game and it'll be as if they dipped themselves in magic waters. The memories will be so thick they'll have to brush them away from their faces…This field, this game: it's a part of our past, Ray. It reminds of us of all that once was good and it could be again."

May it be so.

Fences

Last year my wife and I took a long-awaited pilgrimage of sorts to the red rocks of Sedona, Arizona. Robert Redford says, "Some people have therapists. I have Utah." Cindy and I have Arizona.

On our first morning there, I rose early for a walk, some of that desert stillness, and an exploration of my new surroundings. The Schnebly Hill Formation, that red sandstone that gives Sedona its beauty, was glowing like a furnace as the sun began to rise. The sky was as blue as the turquoise mined from the local soil, and the wind was howling like mad across the desert. It was perfect.

As I walked and uncoiled my mind with coffee in hand, I saw a small church in the distance. It sat there, steeple splitting the sky, nestled in the rocks. It was Sunday, and I thought, "I'll go over there, sit down in the quiet and enjoy the sanctuary." There was only one problem: I couldn't get there.

I tried to walk in a straight line toward the little church but only met concrete and adobe walls, security fences and the like. I took to the local sidewalks. They led to no where. I walked down the road. Nothing but dead ends. Finally, I gave up, refilled my coffee cup in the hotel lobby, and sat down outside to enjoy God's perfectly built house of worship. My inability to get to church got me thinking, though.

Our communities – our world – is filled with people who desperately long to commune with God. They hunger and thirst for a spiritual relationship. They are wasting away, alone in their homes, with no real connection with God or even other human beings. They need faith. They need hope. They need community. They need good news. But they can't get to it. There are just too many barriers. Too many fences. Too many dead ends. And most of these are human-made. So, these seekers just go home, drink their coffee or Scotch or whatever, and try to relate to God alone, with varied levels of success.

But I wonder what would happen if our churches and communities of faith became places that seekers of God could actually get to? Rather than shouting at and condemning people, what if we instead developed the skills of spiritual navigation – pointing people toward faith, not pointing at their faults, and helping those trying to connect with God, actually find him?

What if we began to recognize that Christianity can offer the world more than strong-armed morality or a list of dos and don'ts? Instead, what if we rediscovered the ambition of tearing down the barriers that keep people from God? What if we learned to invite people into the life-changing, life-forming story of what it means to be spiritually alive?

I did an interview recently where the interviewer asked me questions for nearly an hour about what it means to be the church in today's world. I spoke about my Sunday morning walk in Sedona and said, "I'm not very interested in being a part of a church or a religious organization per se; but I am interested in following a distinct way of life, the way of Christ."

She had a hard time understanding this. So I told her about my uncle Lamar. Uncle Lamar has been a Baptist preacher for forty years. And he is the best carpenter in all of Gordon County, Georgia. Now in his mid-70s, he continues to build several homes a year. He has a waiting list longer than the years he will likely live. I spent many of my summers working for my uncle, on his farm and on his worksites. I am not a master builder, but everything I have ever learned about building came not from a classroom or a book, but at his hands – watching, learning, listening, imitating.

This is my hope for the church: To become a place where we can learn to watch, listen, imitate and live like Jesus – the Jesus who tore down all barriers and paved a highway to his Father.

I believe the good news found in the way of Christ is more powerful than the corruption, crises, and disasters of this present world. I believe it is ultimately more powerful than the walls and barriers built by human hands. If it's not, then it would not be worth believing, for it would not be the good news we and this world needs.

Promises Kept

When I met him in the fall of 2005, Joshua Burton was seventy-five years old. On a walker, slowed by age, his caramel skin calloused by years of hard work, he still had the light of life in his eyes. His "girlfriend," Susie Ward was even more energetic. Having surpassed three score and ten years herself, you wouldn't know it. She moved and laughed like a woman half her actual age. The life of the party she was.

After their spouses had died, these two future lovebirds struck up a great friendship and later a great romance. It was their plan to stick together for the remaining years they had on earth. So it was on Monday morning, August 29, 2005.

Josh had spent the previous night before at Susie's. She lived in a sturdy little shotgun house, anchored deep in the Mississippi mud; a house she had lived in her entire adult life. This was the home where she had raised her children and where her first husband had died. This house had survived more than a few Gulf of Mexico hurricanes, including the devastating onslaught of Camille in 1969. But Susie's house did not survive Katrina. Joshua Burton and Susie Ward found themselves in a situation they never anticipated.

As the winds howled and the house shook, Josh swung his crippled legs off the bed in the dark of that morning to look outside. His feet landed in ankle-deep water. Hurricane Katrina had pushed a wall of water miles up the Pearl River, and now it washed over the town of Pearlington, Mississippi, from the north. By mid-morning Josh and Susie were clinging to a porch post treading in eight feet of water.

The two prayed that God would somehow save them. Then, at the point of giving up, when Josh's crippled legs could no longer keep him afloat, a life jacket popped from below the surface. They clung to the bobbing house for the next six hours, and when the waters receded it took rescuers three days to find them. They were taken to separate hospitals, one in Meridian and one in Jackson, and their families, thinking they were both dead, did not find them for two additional weeks.

As Josh and Susie were rescued, they made a promise: "If God will allow us to be reunited, we'll be married and finish our days together." That promise was kept. On a cold December afternoon, as they were handed the keys to their new hurricane Katrina cottage by volunteers from Habitat for Humanity of Walton County, Florida, they voiced their vows of commitment one to the other in the front yard of their new home.

Buster Woodruff, a Walton County builder, rented Mr. Josh's tux and gave Ms. Susie away. I was honored to officiate the ceremony as more than a hundred friends and volunteers – donors, designers, and carpenters – stood on the front porch of that new house as witnesses and participants in a fantastic celebration.

Here was this old man and this old woman, near the end of their lives. Why did they go to all this trouble? Because they could; they were alive. Grace had fallen down on them with the rain that stormy morning as they treaded water. As they said their vows, twenty-five feet from their new home, caskets were still lying on top of the ground, burst open from the flooded cemeteries. More than 30,000 families were still displaced. The local economy was in the toilet.

These two could have sat around in a smelly FEMA trailer and pointed fingers and bemoaned how terrible it was – and it was terrible – inhumanely terrible. They could have assigned blame to this group or that group for why Katrina struck. They could have even shaken an angry fist at heaven and blamed God for taking away more than he should have and putting on them more than they could bear.

They didn't do any of those things. They, and their neighbors who had all lost so much, chose instead to get on with it. They chose to live the life they still had to live; to thank God for what remained, and to steal joy wherever they found it.

So thanks Josh and Susie for showing us the faith to press on in a world not yet redeemed. I hope you have a most happy wedding anniversary.

Ronnie McBrayer

The Monastery Master Mix

This summer I made a visit to a monastery. Not that I'm thinking of taking monastic vows, mind you; no, no, no. Jesus told his disciples that not everyone can live the ascetic life. I'm sure he was thinking of me. But I really looked forward to this visit.

My friends and I toured the grounds and for a short time peered into the lives of these men most dedicated to contemplation, hard work, and spiritual discipline. The hillside surrounding the monastery's abbey was dotted with black cows, hay bails, and fruit trees. Consistent with their particular order, these monks were as good with their agriculture as they were with their theology. Inside, we discovered a further treat: Handmade artwork of all kinds. Beads, bracelets, paintings, stained glass; all of these came from the skilled hands of this community.

And the greatest pleasure of all, these monks cultivated beautiful little bonsai trees – hundreds of them. For decades, this order had been refining their proficiency with these potted plants. Their hard work showed. While I expected the times of prayer, the lit candles, the simple but hardy meals, the ringing of bells, and the burning of incense; I did not expect Angus cows and bonsai trees. It was a surprise.

Something else surprised me: A gift shop. That's right. This monastery, this symbol of the casting off of worldly pleasures, had a mini-variety store right there on campus. It ran with an entrepreneurial spirit that would have awed even Sam Walton. Need some books? They got 'em. Want a new rosary? They will set you up. Got the hankering for some fresh preserves or coffee? Step up to the cash register.

Fruitcake, fudge, icons, note cards, souvenirs, and of course, all the bonsai supplies one needed to start their own nursery at home, could be purchased at the "Abbey Store." These supplies included the "Monastery Master Mix," a complex potting soil designed to grow the best bonsai trees under God's heaven.

Did I mention that the chapel was closed on the day of my visit? See, you couldn't pray at the monastery on this day, but you could visit the gift shop. In fact, every single one of the half-dozen monks I met enthusiastically invited me to do so. There I could pick up a bit of the monastic life and take it back home with me for $19.99 plus applicable local sales tax. And don't worry if you left your wallet at home. The Abbey Store offers an extensive virtual shopping experience for those who cannot visit the monastery personally. Online the monks manage an e-commerce catalog and a bells-and-whistles website complete with the little digital shopping cart and everything. They take all major credit cards and even Pay Pal. How edifying.

I left the monastery feeling less spiritual than I had hoped. Don't get me wrong. I'm not so high and mighty that I would deprive these good men of making a living with their hands. I'm all for that. Nor do I think Christian people shouldn't sell things. I'm a good capitalist. Please, visit my own website and buy my books. But something about these good brothers was out of joint. On one hand they were deeply, deeply traditional; long robes, honest labor, living lives dictated by discipline and ritual. Then on the other hand they were so, dare I say, opportunistic.

One moment I seemed to be conversing with Thomas Merton himself, with talks of prayer, fasting, and readings of the Church Fathers, and the next moment this same man would morph into Elmer Gantry trying to sell me glorified potting soil. It was wacky.

Is there no sacred space left in Creation? Have even monasteries been run-over by the E-bay Express? Does every one offer 90-days-same-as-cash now, even those who follow the order of Saint Benedict?

If someone feels led by God to join a monastery and forsake so much that is wrong with life as we live it, then more power to them. If someone wants to operate a thriving internet business, selling everything from coffee mugs to bailing wire, then by all means do it in style. But maybe – just maybe – a little distance between the two would help.

Don't invite me into a spiritual retreat and seem more concerned with swiping my Visa card than assisting my soul.

Get Out Of The Way

"I am the way, the truth and the life," Jesus said. We Christians are quick to fasten hold of these words. We properly talk about his uniqueness, Jesus' distinctive nature, but maybe we miss the point. Rather than treating Jesus as the way to know and experience God, Christians often speak as if Jesus is standing *in* the way. Our view is not to see Jesus as an open door, but to see Jesus as a roadblock.

"Do you want to get to God? Sorry, you have to go through Jesus."

We pitch this sentiment out there like it is something dreadful. Jesus becomes an irate troll living under a bridge, ready to jump out and devour anyone traveling along the road. But to the contrary, Jesus is an open path, much more open than many of us are ready to accept. Just read about some of the people he hung out with and who were his friends: Extortionists, the non-religious, the oddballs and outsiders, welcomed, they were, into his kingdom.

Jesus hasn't padlocked himself behind a steel and concrete wall, waiting for those with just the right code to get through. His arms are open. His way is open. His heart is open. He invites all who will to come to him and find God; to come to him and discover what life can really be.

Most every day I cross the beautiful Choctawhatchee Bay in the Panhandle of Northwest Florida. Birds, dolphins, jumping fish, boaters and kayakers are usual sites along the way. But to cross the bay, I have to use the Clyde Wells Memorial Bridge. A mile and a half long and hanging there in the blue sky, it is the only way to get my vehicle to the other side. What if I arrived at the foot of the bridge and treated it like a roadblock instead of a bridge?

"Who put this bridge in my way? I'm trying to get to the other side. What am I going to do now? My car doesn't float you know. I guess I'll just turn around and go home."

How foolish would that be? The bridge is there for a reason – to be used. The bridge is not *in* the way. It *is* the way.

We should not speak of Jesus, not even when speaking of his exclusiveness, in such a way that communicates a lack of openness on his part. He invites all to travel with him and through him on the journey to know and experience God. But following Jesus is about much more than getting to the other side (You know, going to heaven when you die). Following Jesus is a way of radical living for today, a life of imitation. As long as we live in a "What Would Jesus Do?" world we can wrestle with hypothetical situations and largely remain who and where we are, safe and sound. But when we start asking, "What did Jesus do?" and "How can we do the same?" well, hold on to your hat because things are going to get willy-nilly.

For instance: Do we forgive others as Christ forgave, even as he forgave those who murdered him? Do we turn the other cheek when we are mistreated? Do we love our enemies? Do we resist violence and power, opting instead for the upside down influence that comes from service and surrender? Are we quick to cast off the allure of wealth, serving God rather than the pseudo-securities of contemporary culture?

Are we accepting of all people – even those radically different than ourselves – and welcome them to God's table? Are we ready to speak the truth about religious hypocrisy, about the abuse of position and privilege, and invite those who long to be set free from all coercion to come to Christ to be set free indeed? If so, then maybe, just maybe, we are ready to begin following this way-maker, Jesus.

This life of Jesus-imitation goes far beyond propositions, creeds, and statements of faith. Such things are largely collections of powerless words on paper. But a way of life, living a life like the one Jesus lived, this is the sort of thing that changes the world. Living like Jesus will pit us against the cultural and religious planet on which we live in some very fundamental ways. But being pitted against these means we have something worth saying and a life worth living; the way and life of Christ.

Old Man River

The kingdom of God. This was Jesus' favorite subject. We find the phrase on Jesus' lips more than a hundred times in the gospels. If forced to parse Jesus' message down to one theme, this would be it. But what is this all-important kingdom of God?

The kingdom of God is God's nation. It is the territory over which God reigns. Where ever he has subjects, where ever he has people, where ever men and women give final allegiance to Christ – there is God's kingdom. Jesus recognized a duality in this kingdom. Yes, it is substantial and real, but it is also elusive and unseen, recognized only by those with eyes and hearts of faith.

That is probably why Jesus described the kingdom the way he did. See, he compared the kingdom of God to a farmer who goes out to plant his crops. Only beneath the surface, quietly and unnoticed, do the kernels break open and grow. He compared the kingdom of God to a priceless buried treasure, hidden and concealed in a field. He said the kingdom was like mixing yeast into a bowl of flour. With a little patience and a little time, the yeast would encompass the whole batch of dough. And Jesus compared it to the growth of a mustard seed. Though small and insignificant at first, ultimately the seed is marvelously transformed into an enormous tree giving shelter and shade.

Whatever this kingdom of God is, and it is more than we can think or imagine, it is something that grows and strengthens only with time. It is not always seen or heard from, not always obvious or observable, but below the surface it is there. And one day it will break open on the world.

If Jesus were here today, telling his stories and yarns, and reaching for pictures that describe the kingdom of God, he might reach for the Mississippi River. "The kingdom of God, to what shall I compare it?" he might ask. "It is like the Old Man River."

The headwaters of the Mississippi River are not what you might expect. Flowing out of a little, glacial lake in the frozen tundra of northern Minnesota is a small rivulet. This stream is so narrow, so shallow, that one can walk across it with water up only to his or her knees. But a drop of water, flowing out of that lake, begins a journey that will carry it more than 2000 miles through the heart of North America to the Gulf of Mexico. And that's not the only drop to make the journey.

If you go hiking in western New York, and a drop of your perspiration hits the ground, that drop will find its way to the Mississippi River and the Gulf of Mexico. If you drop your water bottle while camping in the Grand Teton Mountains of Idaho, those droplets will find the Missouri, the Mississippi, and finally the Gulf of Mexico.

With more than twenty major tributaries, the Mississippi River Basin sustains with its water and commerce more than fifty percent of the American population. The center of this country would be a desert without it. And by the time the Big Muddy reaches Louisiana it is three miles wide, two-hundred feet deep, and moving the mass of a hundred-fifty tractor trailer loads of water every second. But in Minnesota, children can play in it as if it were a mud hole.

So it is with the kingdom of God.

With his creative power and love at work in people, Christ is calling a new world into being, even though it doesn't always look like a new world. People are still hungry. Wars are still fought. Injustice is still tolerated. Spiritual darkness and hardness of hearts still abound. It looks a lot like a mud hole. But this river known as the kingdom of God is gaining momentum. Little drops turn into big drops. Tributaries and rivulets collapse on top of one another. The basin of God's power draws everything to itself until finally this river brings life to the whole world.

What is the kingdom of God? It is a farmer sowing his crop. It is a hidden treasure in a field. It is a growing seed. It is a trickling glacial stream. But more so – surprisingly, deliberately, and unexpectedly – the kingdom is coming.

Holiday Heresy

With Christmas upon us, most every day now my children scream and point at the television like their hair is on fire. Why? Because they see another Chinese-produced gadget, toy, or thingamabob they hope to find beneath the tree on Christmas morning. Granted, my children are products of their environment. On any given day the average American sees thousands of images, commercials, and advertisements that seek to entice the dollars from our wallets.

Many of these are aimed directly at our children, conditioning them for a life of conspicuous consumption. So when the marketing assaults of radio, television, print and the internet are added to the screeching of insatiable children, you'll buy most anything just to get them to shut up.

What happened to the simplicity of the Sears and Roebuck Christmas catalog? Back in the day I would begin carrying it around in October – like a sacred text of scripture. By December its pages were so dog eared it was essentially useless. But don't throw it away. God, please no. It was the only connection I had to my dreams of a happy Christmas, for inside its pages were filled with those magnificent pictures of bicycles, GI Joes, Hot Wheels tracks, and Stretch Armstrongs.

Now, when my own children plead and howl for the latest-and-greatest, I understand. Hopefully, though, I also understand what my parents knew back then: A child does not need everything he or she sees.

Though I hated hearing it, and I heard it often, my mother's favorite mantra, "You're old enough now that your wants won't hurt you," becomes truer every day. I even find myself repeating it, despite the fact that I swore in blood oath I would never say such a thing to my own children. But I think my mother's words are the kind of wisdom that needs to be repeated, because growing older hasn't made many of us very mature. We aren't any different than greedy children. Our wants and wishes are as voracious as any ten-year-old's.

I fear we have all become converts to the most dangerous of American religious convictions. This juggernaut of religion has salespersons and marketers as its clergy, the mall as its house of worship, e-Bay as its daily devotional reading, and possessions as its god. We long and pray for the advent of a messiah who will one day come to save us and our money, bearing the banner of a 50% off sale, with coupons and discounts for all, and no-interest payments until next year. This is the good tidings of great joy we now trust and hope for.

Somewhere in the last century we moved from working in order to live, to working in order to consume. Consumerism – the acquisition of things – has become our most treasured sign of prosperity, our most revered value, our way of bringing meaning to our lives. And at its core, especially during this season of Advent, holding to consumerism as a value to be lived out, is rank idolatry. Our soft lives of narcissism have blinded us to the fact that our chasing after the bits and pieces of a commercial society prevents us from truly following Christ.

Jesus said it was the pagans – PAGANS – who chased after things, possessions, and the like, not those who follow him. We hear those words and then celebrate his birthday by spending money we do not have, on things we do not need, for people we don't even like.

So, I wonder if you will join me in doing something dangerously subversive this Christmas. In fact, this is blasphemous to the American mode of worship, an act of heresy: Instead of spending time and money on what you can get, give up some things.

Get off the materialistic merry-go-round. Abandon the mall. Suspend your online purchases. Lock away your credit cards. Show restraint with your shopping. You may find in letting go of all this for just a little while, a whole new way of living may emerge.

It won't be easy. People will think you a scrooge. They will call you a heretic, one unwilling to conform to the religious order. But that's OK. This may prove even better for your soul than for your budget.

WHY?

On February 15, 1947, Glenn Chambers boarded a plan bound for Quito, Ecuador. He was beginning his career as a missionary to the native tribes there. He never arrived. His plane crashed in the mountains of South America.

Moments before he left the Miami airport he jotted a note to his mother. All he could find to write on was a piece of advertising paper. So, he scribbled his message on the back of the advertisement. By accident or providence, Chambers had picked up an advertisement with a single word on the front. In bold black letters – all caps – was the word, WHY? When his mother opened the letter from her now dead son, the first thing staring at her was not the hurried message of her boy. No, like a haunting voice from the grave it was this one word, WHY?

"Why?" is a question we have all asked. Why do good people suffer? Why was my loved one struck with cancer? Why was my child taken from me? Why did my marriage fail? Why does God seem so far away from me? Why is life so unfair? I suspect we'll continue to ask the question of why for the rest of our lives. Jesus asked the question too. He asked it while hanging on a cross.

"My God, my God, why have you forsaken me?" he cried out in agony.

With those words he joined with the angst and disillusionment of millions who have felt the darkness of divine rejection. This abandonment seemed to be the real suffering of Jesus' execution. Yes, hanging on a stick of wood, being pierced by nails, being beaten by thugs, suffering the paralysis and slow suffocation of the crucifixion was hideously painful. But for Christ, this pain of being separated – deserted – by his Father was crushing.

While the crowd of ridiculers gathered, the God Jesus had always known walked away. The Father forsook Jesus at his time of greatest need. It's important to note that Jesus did not feel forsaken, like many of us do from time to time. No, he *was* forsaken. There is a big difference between the two.

When my boys were younger, one had a hard time learning to sleep in his own bed. Sometimes I would place him in the crib and then go stand in the corner of the room, in the dark. But I wouldn't leave the bedside. I saw every tear. I heard every whimper. I was aware of the fear and struggle. And while I could not be seen or heard, still, I was there. Did my son feel abandoned? Probably so. Was my son abandoned? Absolutely not. There was never a moment when he was alone.

But when Jesus screamed out to his Father, "Why have you forsaken me?" it was not a rhetorical question or a false accusation. It was real. It was painful. It was enough suffering to last for eternity.

In the pain of life – when it all comes crashing in – we often feel abandoned and forsaken by God. But God has abandoned none of us. The last divine abandonment took place on a Friday afternoon on a Palestinian hillside. The best man to ever live was abandoned by God so we never would be. The cross reveals a God who would rather go to hell and eliminate it than send his children there. It reveals a God who when he hears us cry out, "I feel alone" doesn't intellectualize the problem. Rather, he has chosen to identify with this feeling. For he has been there himself.

Dorothy Sayers articulated it so well. She said: "For whatever reason God chose to make man as he is – limited and suffering and subject to sorrows and death – he had the honesty and the courage to take his own medicine. When he was a man, he played the man. He was born in poverty and died in disgrace and thought it well worthwhile."

Yes, we will feel very alone from time to time. But those feelings do not change the facts. God thought you and me worthwhile enough to never leave us or forsake us, but to be with us always, even to very end of the age.

One Hell Of A Sermon

"That was one hell of a sermon, preacher."

So went the word of encouragement passed on to my good friend at the conclusion of an especially inspiring Sunday morning sermon. The young man paying the compliment was a simple diesel mechanic named Terry.

Terry came to church every Sunday with grease under his fingernails; tattoos peeking out from beneath his cut-off sleeves; and the smell of Marlboros heavy on his breath. This didn't mean he couldn't recognize a good sermon when he heard one, even if his praise was a bit unorthodox. Beaming from ear to ear, pumping the pastor's hand, this young man was happy to attend this little church to hear good sermons and pursue his new-found relationship with Christ.

It had not always been so. Terry's story was one of glorious conversion like something you hear from a Billy Graham crusade. Drug abuse, alcoholism, failed relationships: He had suffered from and caused more than his share of disaster. Then, by God's grace, it all turned around. My friend, his pastor, had been instrumental in this transformation. He served as a spiritual guide to Terry, a true pastor, helping him sort out all his past baggage, pointing him forward, and allowing the rough edges to remain. After all, God looks at a person's heart not the grease under his fingernails.

If only people were the same.

One Wednesday Terry was running late for the church's weekly Bible Study. He came straight from work. No shower, no shave, no change of clothes. He came like that old hymn so often sang: "Just as I Am."

A self-appointed delegation met Terry in the parking lot on this particular night. This group told Terry that should he wish to continue to be a part of the church, it was time he learned to dress right, cover those devilish tattoos, and clean up his language. Terry's reaction was expected. He was crushed. Bible in hand he returned to his truck, drove away and never returned. The chances of him ever giving church a shot again are slim to none. Who can blame him?

The pastor, my friend, only discovered the transgression against Terry after the fact, when his usual seat in worship was inexplicably vacant. My friend, to his credit, no longer pastors that church.

The last time we find Jesus in synagogue on the Sabbath, he healed a woman who had been crippled for eighteen years. With just a word and a touch he caused her to regain her lost strength. Those who happened to be in church that weekend were astounded. But this was more than the synagogue attendant could stand. He makes the audacious statement, "There are six days of the week to get healed – not on the Sabbath" (See Luke 13). It's good for people to get well, in other words, but not on Sunday and not in the church house.

A woman who had been broken for eighteen years – eighteen years! – had been healed, and all this man could do was fret over the minutia of keeping the rules. He couldn't celebrate the physical and spiritual deliverance of one who had long suffered. All he could see was the grease under the fingernails of a Nazarene carpenter who had violated the sacred customs of worship.

He rebuked the awe-struck crowd and chided the healed and the Healer. We never find Jesus attending the synagogue services again. Never. Who could blame him?

Question: Why won't some people go to church? Answer: Because they have been. This is no excuse for throwing away spirituality, not in the least. But it is recognition that the church, when it behaves in ways oppositional to its Founder, is its own worst enemy.

Jesus intentionally broke the rules and customs of the religious establishment not for rebellion's sake, but to reveal how preposterous it was to hold to these rules: Choosing to honor the oppressive Sabbath law over celebrating the healing of one of God's children; and running off diesel mechanics whose hearts have changed but who don't dress right on Sunday. This is ridiculous! Actually, it's more than ridiculous. It is sinful.

Those whom "the Son sets free are free indeed," and no amount of religious rule-making manipulation can change that.

Summer

Ten years ago Melinda Mayton was sitting in a small Bible study. As part of the study a question was circulated through the group: What would you do if you were given a million dollars?

That's a great question. Customary answers from the group followed. "I would pay off all my bills," one said. "I would buy my mother and father a new house," another chimed in. "My family and I would travel the world," still another offered. When the question made its way to Melinda she answered, "I would take children with cancer to the beach."

At the time Melinda was an oncology nurse at a children's hospital in Atlanta, Georgia. Every day she saw the overwhelming impact on these children and their families who were grappling with a cancer diagnosis. It was more than physical. Fighting the good fight against disease threatened to tear these families apart. In Melinda's mind, a week of retreat might just do the trick for these precious souls. Let the family recharge their batteries. Let mom and dad rediscover one another. Let the siblings of a sick child get caught up on some parental attention – all while enjoying the beauty of sand, sun, and ocean.

Melinda dreamed of giving parents and children a week without hospital visits, without chemo treatments, without needle sticks and without the financial, emotional, and spiritual exhaustion of fighting cancer. She didn't let the lack of a million dollars stop her. Leaving her successful career in medicine Melinda founded the Lighthouse Family Retreat. Since 1999 she, with a committed group of volunteers, has provided week-long respites for some 500 children with cancer and their families.

Recently I participated in one of these retreats at Seaside, Florida. There were a dozen or so sets of moms and dads and their kids. The children were at all different stages of sickness and recovery. Some were newly diagnosed. Others were cancer free and had been so for months. It was a beautifully diverse group.

In the group was a coltish little girl named Summer. Summer is a ten-year-old from Dublin, Georgia, with the spirit and tenacity of a championship prize fighter. She has a difficult prognosis but you would not know it if you met her.

While at the beach Summer wanted to be baptized. I was honored to lend a hand. She and I stepped into the warm Gulf of Mexico early one morning, surrounded by her family, the participants in the week of retreat, and even a few strangers out for their morning walk.

"I baptize you, my sister, in the name of the Father, and the Son, and the Holy Spirit," I invoked as I dipped her perfectly bald head under the water. She emerged with a million dollar smile to the cheers of the scores gathered on the beach. It was one of the more awesome things in which I have ever participated.

We are tempted to wipe the tears from our eyes and say, "What a nice thing to do because time is running out for this child." But I disagree. Summer's decision was not the decision of one who is dying. Rather, this was a decision of faith and hope, a decision made by someone very much alive. A person doesn't make a commitment to follow Christ without believing she will be there to keep up her end of the deal. She believes in this Christ who calls her to himself; a Christ who can and will do incredible things in her life – because she will let him.

A sporadic blessing. A once-in-a-while epiphany. A blue moon movement of God. That is what most of us are living on. But God wants us to experience so much more. He wants us to experience what "eye has not seen, what ear has not heard, what imagination cannot contain." And we will experience this kind of life, if only we believe and follow. Like Melinda. Like Summer.

I do not know what the future holds for Summer, no more than I do for you or me. But I wish her life. I wish her wellness. I pray that she have many years on this earth living out her faith. Still, even if her time is short, her faith is great. And that faith has made her alive – more alive than many of us ever will be.

Addendum: In the time that this world had her, Summer taught us much. She is now alive and well in the presence of God.

Homesick

This past summer friends of mine sent their eight-year-old daughter to camp. This camp was a primitive affair with lodges, sleeping bags, and creatures of the night. Conspicuously absent were all the comforts of home. Air conditioning, television, soft mattresses, beloved pets, video games, fast-food: Not here. This was the roughing-it world of swarming bugs, cold showers, drill-instructor-camp-counselors, and homesickness. Terrible homesickness.

My friends' nostalgic daughter mailed home a letter worthy of comparison to "Greetings from Camp Hiawatha." It did not begin with, "Hello Mother, hello Father..." No, she cut to the chase: "I wish I was home with you."

The letter, a mere two dozen words, made inquiry about her pet cat and best friend and eloquently concluded, "These tents are hotter than hell at night." Now there's a child longing for home.

Aren't we all longing for home?

The Teacher of the Old Testament wrote, God "has planted eternity in the human heart" (Ecclesiastes 3:11). Inside each of us the Creator has placed a sort of homing device. The coordinates are preprogrammed. Our destination – called heaven or nirvana or swarga or paradise – is a return to the God who made us, for only there are our souls truly at home.

The extraordinary conclusion of the Christian Scriptures is the apocalyptic book of Revelation. While much of the book is perplexing, not all of it is so. Revelation 21 paints a beautiful picture of the future heavens and earth. It is a place where there will be no more tears, no more death, no more crying or pain. There will be no more cold camp showers, no more miserable sleepless nights, no more homesickness.

The earth and heaven will be re-created, made new, made as one. The universe will be washed clean of all that is wrong with it. And it will be a place that we will call home with the God who made us. The writer of the book of Revelation does not invent this scene or these words. Largely he is quoting the Jewish prophets of the Old Testament who a millennia before prophesied the same thing.

The prophets envisioned a world where everything – everything – that is now wrong will be made right. It will be made the way God first made things, when he looked out on his creation and said, "This is very good." This good world that we will call home will have no more kids with cancer. There will be no more looting of the earth's resources. There will be no more broken relationships or failures to forgive. There will be no more government corruption or religious hypocrites.

I will rejoice over the demise of all funeral homes and hospitals. I will celebrate the closure of all courts and police forces. I will cheer with you as the doors are locked on all soup kitchens, all psychiatrists' offices, all environmental protection agencies, and all military installations. Why will such organizations go out of business? Because their services will no longer be needed: Everything will be put back into place.

Of course this all sounds well and good: Perfection, justice, wholeness, a brave new world, all this waiting on some far away horizon. But isn't this a bit like trying to explain the joys of college and career to a kindergartner? Isn't this like telling an eight-year-old that she can survive two weeks of camp without electricity? Relief and home are so far away. Isn't this little more than a teasing mirage in the distance? No, it is not.

If I believe anything at all, I believe this promise of God: That while the world certainly appears to be one long, hellacious night, the cool of morning is coming. Like campers sweating it out in the darkness, we are waiting for the new creation of God to dawn.

Yet, we are not merely marking time. We live with the hope of eternity always before us. We live, no matter the sufferings or injustices we face, knowing that we are just passing through on our journey, aliens and strangers in a strange land. Somehow, all of creation – the heavens and the earth, human beings, all that is – is in process. It is moving toward the destination of renewal and redemption. It is moving toward home, a home where everything will be as it should.

Ronnie McBrayer

Can You Hear Me Now?

I still chuckle every time I hear the story. It seems a poor fellow's vehicle had conked out on the side of the road. After waving about like a banshee for half an hour he finally convinced a speeding motorist to stop and help.

"If you could just push my car at a speed of forty miles per hour," the stranded motorist said to his newly arrived partner, "I'm convinced it will start and I'll be on my way."

Sliding back behind the wheel of his car the driver was relieved. The ordeal of being stuck in the middle of nowhere was finally over. He would be rolling again in a matter of seconds, all his worries behind him. Yes, his worries *were* behind him, for as he waited for that gentle nudge on the rear bumper that would move him down the road, it never came. Looking around he discovered that his Good Samaritan had disappeared.

What a cruel joke! Where could he have gone? It was then that he saw him in the rearview mirror. His rescuer was a quarter of a mile away and bearing down on the broken down car at forty miles per hour. The driver had not communicated as clearly as he had intended.

We Christians tend to bumble our communication a little more than most. In these harrowing days when fewer and fewer people seem to stop and listen to what we have to say, we sometimes think the answer is to scream a little louder. Picket signs.

Demonstrations. Boycotts. Petitions. Displays of righteous indignation accompanied by red faces and bulging carotids. The result is indeed clearer communication. It's clear that we are as mad as hell about something.

Without a doubt most Christians want to see serious change in the world. I do to. I would love to see less violence, greater compassion, a moratorium on our limitless consumerism, and fewer public displays of vulgarity, just to name a few. But the solution is not to meet cultural failures with the equal inadequacies of judgmentalism, revenge, and condemnation.

If in our passion to communicate something we feel very strongly about, said communication becomes hateful, as Christians we have betrayed our message. The path of Christ is to love those whom we consider our opponents. The path of Christ is to engage and pray for our enemies, not kill them. And don't be fooled; our words can be as murderous as flying bullets and hand grenades.

Mahatma Ghandi is a hero of mine. We all could learn a great deal from him. He revolutionized India with his leadership of the Indian Independence Movement, and he perfected the philosophy of non-violent resistance. He met the injustice and oppression of his day with peace, integrity, and quiet resolve.

Ghandi said, "We must become the change we wish to see in the world."

If I want a less violent society, I must become less violent. If I want to experience more compassion, I must become compassionate. If I want less consumerism, I should pull my own leg out of the commercialistic trap more often. If I want to protect my children from overt sensuality, then I should teach them respect for others, the value of a person and the human body, and I should probably turn the TV off after 6:00 PM.

So, if you are one who loves a good boycott, why not take a different tact. A little grace, a truce, a lowering of the weapons might be a great change of pace. Oh, and if you have been on the receiving end of a few displays of virtuous disapproval, cut some slack for your accusers as well.

After all, we're all just trying to get the car rolling again. Confrontation without clear communication is nothing less than a wreck waiting to happen.

Keeping the Faith

For Charles

You never knew my friend Charles. You would have loved him. He was a husband, father, English teacher, social worker, canoeist, bluegrass player, therapist, connoisseur of green-apple moonshine, and a good friend. He spent the last decade of his life as the Director of Student Services in my hometown school district. He was on the front lines of advocacy for some of the most vulnerable children in the community. It was a role he relished almost as much as playing Beatles and John Prine songs.

Charles died a few weeks ago, finally succumbing to his two-year battle with leukemia. Friends of his gathered on a scraggly piece of land along the Tallapoosa River in north Georgia for his memorial service. I am certain that we gathered exactly where Charles wanted us. He loved that piece of land and the river that runs along side it. He used it as a retreat for his body and soul. It was his sanctuary.

I use the word "sanctuary" intentionally, for Charles wouldn't enter a church. See, there was always a rebel's spirit behind Charles' jolly school-boy smile and speckled beard. And that rebel-rousing spirit wasn't always validated.

Charles lost a good deal of faith in politics, in education – in the human race in general. He seemed to lose the most faith in religion. He and I would often speak of music, faith, and religion, and at such times I could always count on him to sum up his approach to worship by quoting Ms. Emily Dickinson.

Some keep the Sabbath going to church; I keep it staying at home;
With a bobolink for a chorister, and an orchard for a dome.
Some keep the Sabbath in surplice; I just wear my wings;
And instead of tolling the bell for church, our little sexton sings.
God preaches – a noted clergyman – and the sermon is never long;
So instead of getting to heaven at last, I'm going all along!

But for all the confidence that Charles lost, he never lost the romanticism of and faith in living in a better world. This was, after all, his vocation, his calling. He wanted life to be better, more just, more whole. While he was often disappointed, it will not always be so.

We often speak of heaven as that faraway place where we will live in the sweet by-and-by. I no longer consider that to be accurate, because heaven is just not that far away. The Christian faith teaches that we will not so much move up and out to an intangible heaven when we die, but that one day, God will come down and take up residence on earth.

Charles was right to consider his slice of soil and water, his river and sky, to actually be a piece of paradise. For one day all of creation will be re-created, it will be made new. The universe will be washed clean of all that is wrong. God will set things right.

Nothing could make Charles, or us, happier. How great it will be to live with him in that coming world where there will be no more suffering or death, no more government corruption, no more religious hypocrites, no more broken relationships: Just beautiful, stress-less days singing our songs and floating on the river that makes glad the city of God.

Charles' life – and ours – is rough, unfair, and sometimes crooked. But God is working off our hard edges. He is preparing us and the universe for a new existence when everything will be "very good" as God first made things.

The most fitting benediction to Charles' life is not a text from the Bible or frail words attempting to honor his life. That benediction belongs to the gravely voice of Charles' favorite artist, John Prine:

While walking out, one evening, not knowing where to go,
Just to pass the time away, before we held our show;
I heard a little mission band, playing with all their might.
I gave my soul to Jesus, and left the show that night.

The day will soon be over, and evening will be done.
No more gems to be gathered, so let us all press on.

When Jesus comes to claim us, and says it is enough.
The diamonds will be shining, no longer in the rough.

Addendum: In part, this article is the eulogy I delivered at the memorial service of Charles Skaggs. He is missed.

Is There Any Hope?

On Saturday, December 17, 1927, the crew of the Navy submarine S-4 was trolling beneath the waters of Cape Cod Bay. They were engaged in routine testing of their vessel. The Coast Guard Cutter Paulding was traveling across the surface doing the same. The vessels never saw each other.

The submarine broke the surface just in time to receive a deathblow from the Paulding. The submarine, with its crew of forty, sank in less than five minutes. It came to rest more than one hundred feet below on the ocean floor. Rescue attempts, though meager and primitive in 1927, began at once. But due to impossible weather, it took twenty-four hours for the first diver to descend to the wreckage.

As soon as the diver's feet hit the hull, he immediately heard tapping. There were survivors, alive, trapped inside. Pounding out Morse code on the hull with a hammer, the diver discovered that six crewmen had survived the collision. Efforts were renewed to reach these men before it was too late. But again, the weather would not cooperate. Every attempt at salvation failed.

With their air supply dwindling, the six survivors tapped out in Morse code a final haunting question, "Is there any hope?" For the crew of the S-4, hope would not come soon enough. It was three months before the Navy sent the necessary pontoons to raise the vessel.

The human species needs a few essential things in order to survive. Without these, life is perilously short. Food: Without it, you will starve in four to six weeks. Water, even more crucial, can be abstained from for only three days before bodily systems begin to shut down. Air: It takes only seven or so minutes before brain damage is irreversible. And hope. No one can live, truly live, a millisecond without it.

Hope is that intangible fuel that moves the human spirit along when life appears untenable; when marriages fail; when sickness invades; or when our financial future collapses. We anticipate – we hope – that somehow conditions will improve. We hope that tomorrow will be brighter. We hope that the future will be different than the present. Hope enables us to face whatever difficulties come our way with a greater measure of resolve.

After all, if we have hope that things will change, improve, or work out, we can endure most anything. If that hope is taken away, our spirits wilt and all resistance collapses. We need hope to live in this world the same way we need oxygen in our lungs.

Is there any hope? I can hear this question echo from this spacecraft we call Earth. By our own experience we find the New Testament to be correct when it says that all of creation groans for renewal and relief. The world hopes for something better. We, a part of this expectant world, do the same. We hope for a better future for ourselves, our children, and our families. Will hope become reality?

In my own faith tradition all hope is fastened to this child we find lying in a Christmas manger. Advent is a season to remember, yes, the coming of the Christ child into the world. But it is also a time to anticipate. Christians gather in houses of worship and around Advent wreaths to reflect upon the day when Christ will come again. A day when all things – all things – will be made new; a day when hope will become certainty, when what we can only pray for now, becomes definite.

When will this blessed hope, the appearing of Christ, materialize? No one knows. Still, God is not slow concerning his promises as some understand slowness. He is patient, wanting all who will to find this hope that sustains the human heart.

In the meantime, we are called to live lives of holiness and anticipation as we look forward to that day and "speed its coming," the New Testament says. That's right: Speed its coming. The arrival of hope depends largely upon us, the decisions we make and the lives we live. Will we live in such a way to bring redemption to the world?

I hope so.

Ronnie McBrayer

The Will And Won't Of God

During World War Two the Nazis set up a particular camp where prisoners were forced to labor amid barbarous conditions. Prisoners were ordered to move a huge pile of garbage from one area of the camp to another. The next day they were ordered to move the pile back to its original location. So began a pattern. Day after day this scene repeated itself. It didn't take long for the impact of this mindless, meaningless activity to surface.

An elderly prisoner had an emotional breakdown. Another began screaming endlessly until he was beaten into silence. A third man, who had endured years of captivity, threw himself onto the camp's electric fence and was electrocuted. In the subsequent days, dozens of prisoners went insane.

Their captors did not care. These pitiful prisoners were lab animals in a sick experiment to determine what happened to people when they were subjected to leading a life without meaning. The obvious result was insanity and suicide. So "successful" was the camp, they no longer needed to use the gas chambers.

In a strange way, this story explains the success of so many books and personal guidance gurus in our country today. The Best Sellers List is laden with the themes of finding meaning and purpose in life. We are told, and it is true, that we must find meaning in life or we risk breakdown and self-destruction.

Keeping the Faith

We Christians are apt to talk about purpose and meaning under the broad umbrella of a single magical phrase: The "Will of God". If I discover "the Will of God" for my life, if I can unlock that door, open that box, uncover that secret, then, armed with divine purpose and meaning, my life will be supremely satisfying.

There is some truth to this. But be warned: God's will doesn't always end with a bulging bank account, a platinum charge card, and a million dollar smile, complete with ongoing teeth whitening treatments. Sometimes the "Will of God" ends in crucifixion. Sometimes the path of meaning and purpose leads to a cross.

Just ask Jesus.

Hours before the crucifixion, Jesus knelt to pray in an old olive grove called Gethsemane. It was a dark, secluded place, almost haunting. And the only thing more somber than the garden was Jesus' disposition. He had come to what A.T. Robertson called the "supreme crisis of his life." If you read the account you hear Jesus' struggle. He's not praying, using trite, churchy language. He's begging God for mercy. The original language of Jesus' prayer on Holy Thursday night is telling: In the Aramaic he addresses God as "Abba."

"Abba" was a word of deep affection. Loosely translated to English it would mean "Papa" or "Daddy." In the first century an orthodox Jew would have never referred to the Almighty in such a casual fashion. But here, in his hour of great need, Jesus full of emotion reaches to strum the heartstrings of God.

Jesus did not want to continue along this path toward Golgotha. He did not want to do the "Will of God." He hesitated and balked. He cried out, to paraphrase, "Daddy, you can do anything – even change your mind about the cross. That's what I wish you would do."

But his prayer didn't stop there. In sublime surrender he submitted to the path God had for him: "If there is no other way than this – going to the limit and then beyond – well, I'm ready. Do it your way."

In the end we all have a single choice between two things – only two. This choice is between who will be in charge of bringing purpose and meaning to our existence. Will it be us, the creations? Or will it be God, the Creator? Jesus opted for the latter, even though the result was unequaled suffering. He modeled for us the life of purposeful, willing surrender when he said, "Not my will God, but your will be done."

God's will for Jesus was not the assumption of Joseph's carpentry business back in Nazareth. It was not a legion of warring angels sent to deliver him. It was not a long life of populist preaching and wonder-working tent revivals. God's will was the Passion of Good Friday, and the prayer God answered was to give Jesus the resolute strength and grace to face what lay ahead.

I pray he gives us all the same.

Fools And Drunks

Marvin had spent more than two weeks in the hospital trying to clear up a clogged lung. When the final test results arrived, he had more than respiratory issues. He had cancer. Marvin wasn't surprised.

I visited him as he recovered from the minor surgery that placed a plastic tube into his chest. This tube will deliver the cancer-killing chemicals to his malignant lung. And while the treatments will not cure Marvin, these will give him a few more months.

"Look here chaplain," he greeted me holding the end of his newly inserted chemo-line. "They can plug me right in to the cappuccino machine now! I don't even need a cup." We had a great laugh, and since it was early in the morning, we spoke of lattes, espresso, and how decaffeinated coffee was a waste of otherwise good water.

"Let me tell you a story," my friend said. So I pulled up a chair. On previous visits, Marvin had begun to weave the tapestry of his life for me. He had recounted a number of very bad decisions. He spoke of terrible mistakes. And he shared regrets over a life of addiction and squander.

"I was hung over one Sunday morning when my friends came to get me to help them find a lost canoe in the river. We went down to the river, and like fools, plunged in without a thought. It wasn't long until they were all asleep on the bank, exhausted. But I kept looking for that little red canoe. By myself in the river I got caught in a vortex, and it sucked me under the water.

"I fought for what seemed like an hour, but I know now it was only for a few minutes. I could see daylight, but couldn't reach it. I knew I was going to drown. It was then God spoke to me: 'Son, go on down,' He said. But I kept fighting. He spoke again, 'Son, go on down.' Finally, with water filling my lungs I gave up and let the vortex suck me down into the river. I popped right out on the surface and just feet from the bank and lived to fight another day."

Marvin just looked at me for a long time. I dared not speak. When he broke the silence he said, "I guess it's true. God looks out for fools and drunks; because I've been both of those."

Marvin will not be cured, but he sure is getting well. He's healing. There is a difference between the two, you see. A cure is a quick fix, an alleviation of suffering, an elimination of symptoms. A cure will help the body and might add days to life. But getting well, healing, being made whole – this is deeper. Getting well allows one to transcend their sufferings. It empowers the sick to live, even if their disease is never abated. Getting well may not help the body, but it can restore the soul. Marvin is getting well.

Jesus encountered a man not unlike Marvin. The man had been an invalid for nearly forty years, living a life of limitation. Jesus asked him one question: "Do you want to get well?"

The man immediately began speaking of his powerlessness, his useless body, his lack of assistance with his disease and with a cure. Jesus ignored these protests and told the man to "rise and walk." He was cured, but as the story unfolds, he was also made well. He leaves the pages of the New Testament testifying to the transformation that had overtaken him; a transformation that reached far beyond the physical.

My buddy Marvin left the recovery room testifying himself, about a restored faith in people, in himself, and in his God. I refused to entertain the notion that he was "terminal." At that moment, with a new diagnosis of cancer and difficult days of treatment ahead, he was very much alive and well.

I hope I get a few more visits with Marvin before his Ultimate Healing. I want to hear more of his stories. I want to learn, once again, of the relentless pursuit of God's grace. And I want to scrape together the clues of how we can all be healed.

"God looks out for fools and drunks." He sure does, Marvin. He sure does.

Addendum: I did get several more visits with Marvin before his death in the summer of 2007. His "healing" had continued. He whipped his addictions and reconciled with his family. His sister and parents were with him when he died.

PROVERBS

Some Assembly Required

Do you know the three most frightening words in the English language?

"Some assembly required."

You order something online; a toy or a bicycle for your children. Or you go to a big box store to get a grill or piece of patio furniture. When UPS brings it to your door or you find the item you're looking for in the store, it's not ready to go like you saw in the online catalog or the advertisement in Sunday's paper. No, no, no. "Some assembly required," the tag on the box says.

So, you lug this box the size of a queen-sized mattress out to the garage and open it up. You spill out bucketfuls of screws, connectors, rods, and unidentifiable small pieces of plastic that you will never use no matter what the directions say. And for the next six weeks you attempt to put this thing together. The worst case for me was construction of the dreaded children's play set. Child's play it was not.

When I was growing up our swing sets were just tubes of light weight aluminum. If you were swinging too high the front side of the entire swing set would rise off the ground a solid foot. Now, we have these play sets made of concrete anchored, sequoia-like treated timbers and screws the length of baseball bats. Assembly requires the assistance of a civil engineer and a Masters degree from MIT.

When I bought one of these behemoths for my children I was in the back yard with a slide rule and a skill saw for the entire summer. And I lost all credibility with my neighbors. There was no way they were going to this pastor's church, not with the raging four-letter obscenities flying out of my mouth.

When we moved, to my children's chagrin, I left the play set there; not so much as a gift to the family that bought our house. There was just no way I was going to disassemble it and attempt to put it back together again. Once was more than enough. It was too much work.

Some assembly required: This is true of the products you buy, the relationships you have, the children you are raising, and the kind of person you are becoming. We are all works in progress, even as this relates to our faith. The Apostle Paul said to the Philippians: "Continue to work out your salvation."

We have been given this wonderful gift of grace – the gift of salvation. Christ has redeemed us, calling us to himself to follow and imitate him. This gift is like getting a bicycle in a box. It's like owning a swing set, but the materials are stacked up in the back yard. It's like possessing a new piece of patio furniture but it's actually in a half dozen pieces.

You've got to work it out. You've got to put it all together. You can't ride the bike if it stays in the box. You can't play on the swing set if it remains disassembled. You can't enjoy your patio furniture if you don't connect the pieces. And faith will not be what it is intended to be – what God wants it to be in your life – if you don't work it out, if you don't open the box and put it all together.

Maybe faith has become such a misery – a burden – for some of us because we're lugging around on our backs the box full of assorted spiritual materials rather than putting it all together. The reading of Scripture, prayer and fasting, meditation and retreat, good works done in the name of Christ, service of the poor, worship, periods of contemplation and reflection, times of doubt and frustration: Somehow these all come together to shape and make us who we are. Somehow these things become transformational in our lives. Somehow these pieces fit together to form something useful, something valuable, something that looks a lot like faith.

So pop the bands on that box that's been waiting for you in the garage. Put on your work gloves and break out the tool chest. Call your neighbor to lend a hand. Before you know it, all the pieces will fall right into place…maybe.

Ronnie McBrayer

What Do I Turn Now?

Jesus said, "If someone slaps you on the right cheek, offer the other cheek also." These are some of the more knotty and uncomfortable words Jesus ever spoke. He seems to imply that his followers should be something like sponges. Our only response to injustice, we have sometimes been led to believe, is to grin and bear it.

When we are struck by a fist on the playground, we are to just take it. When sharp words lodge in our hearts at the workplace, we are to silently go about our business. When a violent husband assaults his wife in the bedroom, she should just accept it. I don't think this is exactly what Jesus is saying, not in the least.

There is a subtle but important word in Jesus' command that his original hearers would have understood well. It has been lost in translation to us. It is the word, "right." If someone slaps you on the "right" cheek, offer the other one also. Being struck on the right cheek was a description of someone getting backhanded, not someone in a fistfight. A strike on the right cheek was an act intended to humiliate, used by someone in power over someone who was powerless or vulnerable.

It was how a master would treat a slave or a landowner would treat a sharecropper. It was the common approach of the Roman soldier in his treatment of the Jewish citizenry. It was how many a husband behaved toward his wife in that very chauvinistic culture.

When facing this kind of unjust humiliation, Jesus proposes neither an act of violent retaliation nor a humiliated cowering on the ground in submission. He offers a third way: Turn the other cheek. Rob the aggressor of his power to disgrace you. By offering the other cheek the Christian says to his or her antagonist, "I refuse to be humiliated. Try again."

This is a nonviolent, dignified resistance that exposes the act as unjust, and turns the shame back on the perpetuator of the violence. This kind of peaceful, though uncompromising response, trumps the violent power of the world. By turning the other cheek the Christian is saying, "I will not lift a finger to hurt you in retaliation, but I will never back down from what is just and right."

When I was in middle school we were always getting in trouble during P.E. I don't know why; because in those days, not that many years ago, troublesome boys were not sent to In-School Suspension or assigned to detention. The coach took you over to the water fountain. You gripped the sides of the thing, gritted your teeth and said your prayers as he commenced in lifting your heels off the ground via your backside with a wooden paddle. That was bad enough. But if you cried in front of your friends or the girls, well, it was an embarrassment worse than death.

On one particular day a fellow classmate of mine was accused of stealing something from someone's locker. Before we knew it he was being dragged away to the gallows, uh, the water fountain rather, to face the consequences. Now, this kid was no angel, but we all knew he didn't do it. Not this time anyway. It seems that everybody knew he was innocent of the charges except the coach. When the boy got to the fountain of punishment he did something extraordinary – especially for a middle-schooler.

He dropped his gym shorts right there in front of everyone, including the girls who have such a magical power over adolescent boys, and he shouted in his skivvies, "I have nothing to hide. If you're going to paddle me, it will be like this!" The coach couldn't deliver the punishment.

The boy was wise beyond his years. He didn't launch into a verbal tirade, take a swing at his accusers, or threaten to bring his parents to the school. Nor did he grovel on the floor and take the paddling as if he were guilty. He turned the other cheek – every cheek he had, actually.

We are called to turn the other cheek, not because it always works to disarm injustice, or because it is always practical, but because it is the way of Christ. In following this way, it gives God the opportunity to act and speak in ways we cannot yet imagine.

Strike Three, Surdykowski, Strike Three

Before her retirement, my friend Betty Ann worked for the tourist development council of my hometown. She was the convention and visitors director. God must have a sense of humor. Let me explain.

As she and her family unpacked in the sprawling metropolis that is Calhoun, Georgia, it didn't take long for her new neighbors to arrive with the welcome wagon. Betty Ann was asked the normal "get-to-know-you" questions which basically consist of "Who's your mama?" and "Where do you go to church?" The answer to those two questions pretty much determines one's fate in the small country towns of the Bible Belt. Betty Ann's answers made her a strange animal indeed.

First, she and her family were not from here; "here" being inside the confines of the Gordon County line, established 1850. Anyone outside those boundaries was a foreigner. Betty Ann was a sojourner from points far above the Mason-Dixon Line. Yes, she was a Yankee. Second, Betty Ann didn't have a "normal" last name like Greeson, or Carson, or Wilson. No, her last name was Surdykowski. It didn't matter that she was born with the last name O'Reilly. Her husband had "ski" on the end of his name. She was Polish and that was that.

As the gals from the welcome wagon headed for the door after their first visit, they were in deep contemplation over this new woman in town. One turned just before crossing the threshold and asked, "I have one more question. Are you also…Catholic?" Strike three.

That's right. Betty Ann Surdykowski, director of tourism for a town whose premier annual event is a Civil War reenactment, was a Yankee, Polish, and Catholic. God is still laughing at this most un-Southern trifecta.

But the town gave Betty Ann a shot. I'm glad. We found her to be a lovely woman: Smart, funny, well-connected, a wife and mother. Everyone came to know this about her. Our lives were greatly enriched because she dared to journey into the hills of Appalachia.

In the Good Book Jesus said, "Do not judge others and you will not be judged. For you will be treated as you treat others."

Why does Jesus always complicate our lives with sayings like these? And more than complicate, this strikes at the heart of what we do best: Critique other people. You know it's a favorite pastime, and we all participate. We do it at the mall, the theater, the beach. We call it "people watching." As the public parades by we sort them into categories like dealing cards. We look at the color of their skin, the number and location of their tattoos or piercings, the ethnicity of their last name, their nationality, neighborhood, or religion. Then, we are able to pigeon-hole them rather quickly, and draw the lines that separate us.

"Oh, I'm not judging others," a good Christian might say. "Jesus said we would know people by the fruit they bear. I'm just a fruit inspector." A fruit inspector, you say. Since when did God authorize us to make his management decisions?

There is enough separation in the world: Democrat versus Republican, Christian versus Muslim, White versus Black, Male versus Female, North versus South, East versus West, Haves versus Have-nots, Protestant versus Catholic. The church is called to a different kind of existence.

The church is united not by race, color, creed, nationality, ethnicity, or socio-economic standards. We are united by the body and blood of a crucified and risen Jesus. The New Testament church was and remains the only society in which rich, poor, slaves, masters, the hungry, and the full could come together as equals without prejudice.

Without prejudice? What would that world look like? A world without narrow-mindedness, bigotry, or intolerance; a world that does not size up others based on the town of their birth, the accent with which they speak, or the shape of their house of worship: That world would look a whole lot like the kingdom of God.

Our neighborhoods are filled will Betty Ann Surdykowskis – people we think so different than who we are. Give them a chance. You will find they aren't that unusual after all. You will find new friends. You will let go of some of the prejudices that have kept your world so small. And you just might enjoy a slice of how things were made to be.

Warning: This Is Controversial

Going to bed a few nights ago, my son asked a question that only nine-year-olds can produce out of thin air: "Does everybody who goes to war die?" I quickly answered, "No!" and gave him as much assurance as I could as he scampered up his bunk-ladder to bed. After I left his room, I knew my answer had been a lie.

Everyone who goes to war, in fact, dies. Some die physically. Others are maimed or crippled. Still more come home suffering the lifelong ills of post-traumatic stress disorder and other mental illnesses. All lose time that would have been spent with family, friends, children, and lovers. All have something taken from them: Innocence, hope, or their future. So all who go to war, contrary to the bedtime answer I gave my son, die.

The next day my son came rushing through the house with a beach bucket on his head, a book bag strapped to his back, his imagination obviously running wild. "What are you doing?" I asked. "Going to war," he said.

It stopped me cold. I took the bucket off his head, gathered him into my arms and said, "Son, I pray you never have to go to war." With a casual smile and wave of his hand he said, "Oh, don't worry, Dad. That will never happen."

I hope he's right; but statistics aren't on his side. In the history of recorded civilization there have been less that two hundred years of actual peace among nations, tribes, and people groups. The rest have been engulfed in combat. How do we counter such a dominant worldview; such a controlling theme that has dictated most of human history; this fascination with killing our enemies?

I hate simplistic answers, and while this might sound like one, it's certainly not: We must take the words of Jesus seriously.

This season of the year we gather around the manger that holds the Prince of Peace but fail to hear his words. It was he who said, "Love your enemies, do good to those who hate you, bless those who curse you, and pray for those who mistreat you." We Christians are very good at praying, going to church, planning meetings, and handing out our propaganda. But we have not been very good at taking Jesus' words about peace and nonviolence to heart.

I write and speak regularly on a wide variety of topics. This one subject – waging peace rather than waging war – always generates the most controversy. I would get less heat if I slandered the Virgin Mary or burned Bibles in the street. Why is this? It is because we believe a lie. We believe that violence can somehow save us. We believe that killing will lead to less killing. We believe that warfare will produce peace. In short, we trust the way of the gun more than we trust the words of Jesus.

When confronted with this, well, it makes us mad. But I can't blame anyone for getting angry. I don't like it either. Because I see what such talk earned Jesus: A cross. And if we take the words and actions of Jesus seriously, imitating him, we just might earn the same. Our peacemaking might get us killed, or marginalized, or our e-mail inbox filled with hate mail. Who knows? But I do know this: If we think we will protect our children, our future, and our way of life by killing those who threaten us, we have a poor understanding of history and an even poorer understanding of what it means to follow Jesus.

Now, I know these are dangerous words. Just by jotting them on paper I can feel the lunge of being thrown into a collision course with the values of our society. But the values of our society and the values of Christ, contrary to some opinions, do not always intersect. To love our enemies and work for peace is not efficient, easy, or popular. But it is right. It is redemptive. It is the kingdom of God. And while it appears desperately foolish – foolish enough to put you on a cross – we must remember that the way of Christ involves much more than a baby in a manger.

Ronnie McBrayer

The Gospel According To Rwanda

For the last century or so, Christians in the West – in Europe and the United States – have been taking Christianity to the world in an unprecedented manner. One area where Christian missionaries have had their greatest "success" is central Africa, particularly in the country of Rwanda.

By the early 1990s, after a hundred years of Christianization, eighty percent of the Rwandan populace was "Christian." Rwanda became a missionary case study in achievement. On any given Sunday, seventy-five percent of Rwandans were sitting in a Christian church. Then, in 1994, a civil war erupted in that country, pitting the Hutu tribe against the Tutsi tribe. Over the course of three months nearly one million Tutsis were murdered in a brutal genocide.

Rob Bell reports that some Hutu congregations left their churches after Sunday worship, armed themselves with machetes, and hacked to death Tutsi congregations who were huddled for safety in their own churches. We who live in a sterile and civilized society are quick to condemn this kind of atrocity, as rightly we should. We who are Christian protest further and object, "Those people who committed these killings did not believe the gospel. There is no way a person can truly be a follower of Christ and do such horrible things." And those protests would be absolutely correct. But the confession of faith professed by the Rwandan majority was the same professed by many in the West. After all, from whom did they learn to believe?

What if a survey was conducted of those leaving our American churches one Sunday? What if that survey involved a single question: "What is the gospel that Jesus preached?" The answer, very likely, would be a consistent one. That answer would go something like: "Jesus died on a cross for my sins. If I invite him into my heart I will be forgiven and get to go to heaven when I die." There would be some variation but not much.

This is the gospel we typically preach, the gospel we typically believe, and the gospel we take to the world. This is the belief of many Rwandans and Americans alike. Sadly, it is a confession of faith that is grossly disconnected from the world in which we live. It is a confession focused almost entirely on the next life – as if this life matters little, if any at all.

But is this what Jesus himself preached as he appeared in the deserts of Galilee? I don't think so. The gospel that Jesus preached was the good news that the kingdom of God had arrived. It was not a place. It was not about getting your ticket punched so you were guaranteed a seat on the bus that would take you to heaven when you die. Rather, Jesus' message was that the rule of God had been brought to bear in the present world. "God has moved into the neighborhood," to use Eugene Peterson's vivid phrase; and business as usual will no longer be usual.

Even the Lord's Prayer affirms this gospel: "Thy kingdom come, thy will be done on earth, as in heaven." As Jesus prayed, the objective was not to get to heaven, but to ask that the rule of heaven be brought to earth. This is the gospel. Does this mean there is no meaning in "asking Jesus into your heart?" Is there no meaning in individual salvation? I'm not saying that at all. But an understanding of the gospel that concerns itself only with getting my own soul into heaven – damn this world, it's all going to burn anyway – falls miserably short of the revolutionary message of Jesus.

Jesus did not come to live in your heart like an imaginary friend to keep you company or hold your hand when you are afraid. He came to bring you into the kingdom of God that you might be a part of God's ministry of justice and mercy. He came, not to give you peace about the afterlife per se, but to revolutionize the life you live today. Any gospel that separates today from eternity is not the gospel. Any profession of faith that sanctions the abuse of others or this creation, is a profession of exploitation, not faith. And those who follow a Christ who concerns himself only with the hereafter, are not following Christ at all.

McDonaldization

"**McDonaldization.**" I love that word. It was first coined by sociologist George Ritzer to describe American culture. The predictable, robotic means of producing hamburgers and fries, according to Ritzer, has overtaken our society. Like one giant automated system everything from fast food to childcare to education rolls off the assembly line to be delivered to the consumer for the saving of time, money, and effort.

Ritzer contends that what is saved by means of efficiency is lost in taste, creativity, and naturalness.

Scottish theologian John Drane has rightly applied the term to contemporary spirituality. For the most part, he says we have lost our spiritual imagination and daring. I think he's right. I also think McDonaldization applies specifically to the American church. We have so motorized, organized, and institutionalized the church that songs, sermons, programs, and prayers just roll off the spiritual assembly line. The religious consumer can then peruse the products and hopefully make their purchases.

Churches have become chains or brands, where if you've been to one, you been to them all. Every movement and word is orchestrated to ensure the customer is guaranteed a consistent experience. The production is the most important thing, even if creativity and authenticity must be sacrificed in the process. What are actually produced are churches where appearance is more important than substance. Sound-bite, quick-fix consumers are targeted at all cost. Don't risk the customer going down the street to another spiritual one-stop-shop that offers all the latest products and services with a thirty-day-money-back guarantee if not completely satisfied.

As Christians we want so much for our churches to "succeed" that we will go along with most anything the culture decides is successful. Whatever will draw a crowd, whatever will fill the offering plates, whatever will keep people in the pews. These we will embrace without discretion or good judgment.

After all, if the goal is the make the church bigger and better, then this is what we should do. Raise the sanctified golden arches and use whatever method will ably deliver the goods to the religious shopper. Just get the right preaching, the right music, adequate parking, proper advertising, the most alluring programs. Then people will surely flock to the campus. It is a "build it and they will come," approach to faith. But is this even the point?

What if efficiently "succeeding" isn't the goal at all? What if having the biggest and finest crowd isn't the primary objective? What if our carefully controlled, mass produced spirituality ends up being a distraction to true growth?

Instead, what if the goal is for us to learn to be partners together on this journey of following and becoming like Christ? What if the goal is to be the unique, counter-cultural, community of God? What if the goal is to love our neighbor and aid people in becoming who they were created to be? Then, with all our big plans and strategizing, we probably have our ladder propped up against the wrong wall. While the culture around us can cookie-cutter its marketing plan to draw the biggest crowd, this does not mean the same practice is right for the church.

Now, I am not suggesting that our churches should be anti-growth or that they will not be places full of life and growth. I am not saying that at all. On the contrary we may be fortunate enough to have an abundance of energized, fellow-travelers on this journey. Yet, I am saying this: Churches should cease in their efforts to build spiritual shopping malls and focus instead on helping people become committed followers of Jesus. This may reduce our attendance numbers and the financial bottom line, but without a doubt this will increase our distinctiveness, and certainly our credibility.

For Jesus did not teach, bleed and die to give birth to just another American McDonalds-ized corporation concerned with expanding its market share. Jesus bled into existence his own body, the church. Consequently, the church does not have a product to sell or merchandise to pitch to would-be consumers.

Spirituality cannot be mass produced, wrapped in wax paper, and put under a heat lamp. Genuine spirituality must become a way of living; an alternative lifestyle; a collection of people who become what Jesus is.

Sprinkles

My three-year-old son, Braden, and I sat together one evening watching his favorite channel: The Cartoon Network. I must admit I found myself chuckling a fair amount at the antics of all those animated characters. It wasn't Bugs Bunny or Huckleberry Hound, but it was entertaining enough.

After a few laughs Braden reached up with his small hands and rubbed the skin around my eyes and temples. He burrowed his chubby little fingers into the ever deepening crows' feet that now mark my face. Just as I was about to push his aggravating hands away, he asked, "What are those?" My laughing stopped immediately.

Despairingly, I said, "Those are wrinkles."

A few days later Braden and I were buzzing down the highway, he sitting in his car seat in the back of our family SUV. Out of nowhere he said to me, "Dad, I don't have any sprinkles." I looked in the rearview mirror to find him carefully rubbing his temples. I laughed hard, showing off my "sprinkles" once again.

"Why do I have sprinkles," I asked my observant son, bracing myself for the answer. Surely if he has noticed my wrinkled face he has also made note of my now graying beard, expanding love handles, and aching joints. But his answer was a pleasant, most unexpected surprise. He said, "Because you need sprinkles to help you smile." And smile I did.

One of my favorite pictures of Jesus has him seated on a big Palestinian rock. The artist, unknown to me, has surrounded him with smiling, playful children. The Son of God, head thrown back in laughter, is smothered with little ankle-biters of all nationalities, races, and colors. That portrait comes right off the pages of the Gospels. People were bringing their children to Jesus to be touched and blessed by him. Jesus' disciples, with no tolerance for such immature distraction, began running off the children and their parents. Jesus rebuked the disciples strongly, and readily invited the children into his arms.

He also took the opportunity to be instructive. He said, "Unless you become as a little child you will not enter the kingdom of God." Strangely, Braden reminded me of that picture and the words of Christ. We grown-ups worry over so many things: Our finances, politics, the stock market, the color of the new carpet in the church sanctuary. We fret over our weight, our wrinkles, what sags and sways on our bodies. We have built up defense mechanisms to protect ourselves from others and the world. In the process, we miss out on so much. Children have no such concerns or inhibitions.

Blissfully, children live their lives with abandon. They soak up every moment of happiness. They quickly forget pain and heartache. They deal honestly and lovingly with those around them. They collapse into their beds at night, exhausted, having lived another day to its fullest. And they awake in the morning, slate wiped clean, ready for a new adventure.

Children attack life with the passion of a zealot, the love of heaven, the forgiveness of a saint, and the nakedness of an open book. Jesus was right to point us toward the little people in our lives. How I wish we adults could live with the same state of mind!

My wish can become reality, I think. A child, no matter his or her age, is one who is still learning, still dependent, one who has not lost the God-given gift of trust. A child is one who still has an impressionable mind and a pliable will. One can live as a child whether he or she is seven or seventy years of age.

Brennan Manning is right: "Heaven will be filled with preschoolers. No adults will be allowed admittance."

Heaven is only for those who are still in diapers; only for those who still have a sense of openness and adventure; only for those who still reach out to touch the faces of those they love; only for those with the openness and sincerity of youth; only for those who will allow God to actually do something with them.

Heaven waits for those children of all ages who possess a curious, welcoming smile – even if that smile is surrounded by sprinkles.

Keeping the Faith

My Jesus Is Better Than Your Jesus

Reverend Ken Autry is the former pastor at First United Methodist Church on the lake yard in DeFuniak Springs, Florida. I say, "former" pastor only because he has now moved on to another appointment. Those Methodists won't let their preachers sit still for very long.

He once shared a letter with his congregation that I have yet to get out of my mind. The letter, while not written to Rev. Autry, had been written by a parishioner who had become quite disgruntled with her pastor. This is not uncommon. Sometimes there is the perception that those of the cloth should be absolutely faultless. When failures occur, and they certainly will, the fallout can be crushing. This is too bad. Sure, there are some bad apples in the barrel, but most pastors, priests, and rabbis are doing the best they can to honor their calling and to help others. They make mistakes, but don't we all.

This particular church member gave no quarter for such ministerial blunders. With teeth on edge she poured out a venomous letter to her pastor. She recounted his failures. She demeaned his family. She compared him to other great pastors that had gone before him (always good for your self-esteem), and pretty much read him the riot act.

It was the conclusion of the letter that still rings in my ears. She wrote, "I pray that you will come to know Jesus as *I* do, rather than just knowing Jesus like *you* do."

When we need ammunition against our enemies, any bullet will do. Even Jesus. Since his incarnation Christ has taken on any and every form we require of him. The zealots of his time wanted him to be a revolutionary with sword in hand. The legalists tried so very hard to make him a traditionalist. The anxious masses, and those closest to him, attempted to make him king of Israel.

Satan himself even got in on the act. He invited Jesus to seize economic, religious, and political power. Christ, of course, rebuffed all these efforts. In fact, Jesus' eventual crucifixion was due largely to the fact that he would not play by the rules. He would not be the kind of Messiah people thought he should be. He would not conform.

We continue the tradition. If needed, we will wrap Christ in the red, white, and blue and send him out before our armies waving the flag. We will use his words to strengthen capitalism and justify our greed. We will explain away his hardest sayings in order to get cozy with him. We'll even drop his name in the right circles if it will garner a few more votes in November. Yes, it seems we've got Jesus right where we want him: Shrink wrapped, canned, freeze dried. In an emergency just add water.

The Jesus who walked the Palestinian hills of the first century was a far cry from these things. Certainly he would have shocked us. The calloused hands of a carpenter; the olive skin of the Middle East; the dirty feet, shaggy hair, and tattered clothes of an impoverished gypsy: He is nothing like the white, middle-class, blue-eyed Jesus that appeared on my Sunday school flannel graph board.

I admit I don't always recognize Jesus. Just when I think I have him figured out, he does something crazy: Like command me to love my enemies; or tell me to do good to those who don't deserve it; or challenge me to give away my possessions; or instruct me to turn the other cheek; or allow himself to be crucified, only to rise from the dead. In his unconventional, eccentric manner he runs roughshod over my preconceptions. He overturns the established order of my life. He surprises me with his fierce grace. He calls me to himself demanding my soul, my life, my all.

Jesus asked his disciples on his last night on earth, "Do you not yet know who I am, even after all the time I have been with you?"

I am afraid the answer is still an embarrassing, "No," regardless of spiteful letters from unhappy church members. But thankfully, we'll have all of eternity to get to know this wild-eyed Jewish rabbi a little better. Maybe, just maybe, that will be time enough.

Which Path To Peace?

"Glory to God in the highest, and on earth peace, good will toward men." So the angels sang on Nativity's morning. Peace on earth? We haven't seen much of that. In the course of written human history, there have been nearly 15,000 recorded wars and less than two centuries of peace. Modern, civilized times have not improved the statistics. Of all the people ever killed in conflict between nations, 90% have been killed in the last one hundred years. The last century was the most advanced and most Christian in history. Yet it was also the most violent; a far cry from the angelic chorus.

Jesus said in the Sermon on the Mount, "You have heard the law that says, 'Love your neighbor' and hate your enemy. But I say, love your enemies! Pray for those who persecute you! If you love only those who love you, what reward is there for that? If you are kind only to your friends, how are you different from anyone else?"

In the face of military might, with a terrorist in every airport, nuclear weapons testing in Asia, and atomic ambitions in the Middle East, we are tempted to completely disregard Jesus' words. Isn't it useless to love your enemies in the context of a violent world where you must kill or be killed, where you must get them before they get you? If we follow Jesus here, wouldn't we compromise our way of life, our security and safety, and our well-being? But it is here that we arrive at the root of the problem: War and violence do more than take the lives of people. These take away our faith.

War promises us something we all deeply desire, something we want more than violence: Peace. War promises us, that in the end, when the last battle is fought and the last enemy is slain, we will have what we always dreamed of – utopia, prosperity, safety, a world without suffering, death or bloodshed; a world of peace.

Yet, these are the very things Christ offers with the kingdom of God. A world where the lamb will lay down with the lion, a world where swords are beaten into plowshares, a world where mercy and justice flow down like the waters, a world where every tear will be wiped away from our eyes, a world where there will be no more death or sorrow or crying or pain.

Christ and violence offer the same thing. The two are competitors for our allegiance, and when we resort to violence, even to combat violence, we have left the path of Christ. We are trusting war to save us, to redeem us, and we are failing to trust Christ to keep his word to do the same. We are failing to follow the Christ child who came as the Prince of Peace.

How then should we live? William Willimon makes a great suggestion. As a starting point, if we can't seem to love our enemies, then why can't Christians at least agree not to kill other Christians? We are of the same family, worship the same Lord, we are bound together by the same blood. Would that not be a great place to start?

"I'll do what I can in the cause for security and for justice, but I'll do nothing to endanger my fellow Christians." What if that became the sentiment of followers of Christ? From there, it's not a hard stretch to imagine Christians actually committing to not kill any other human being.

We cannot expect this fanatical idea of Jesus to be accepted by everyone. But Christians should wrestle with these words and hopefully, eventually, submit to them. Why? Because our allegiance is not, first and foremost, to a flag, to a country, to a military, or to a nation. Our primal allegiance is to the Christ child lying in manger and who now rules from heaven.

Oddly enough, this talk of peace may put us at odds with our neighbors, but hopefully it will put us in step with the person of Christ, who came to bring "peace on earth and good will to all."

God @#%!

When I was growing up, church for me was not a social activity. It was not a weekly event or a spiritual distraction to assist you with the trials of life. Church was a non-negotiable obligation. Sunday School, Sunday morning preaching, Discipleship Training, Sunday night worship, Monday night youth group, Wednesday night prayer meeting, choir rehearsals, revivals, tent-meetings, on and on: I had a drug problem from a very early age. I was drug to church every time the doors opened.

As the great Ferrol Sams puts it: "It was imperative that one be Saved. It was just as important to be Raised Right. The child who had been Raised Right was not only Saved but had spent a large part of his formative years in the House of the Lord. Methodists probably could be Saved, but there was a question whether any of them really had been Raised Right."

A part of being Raised Right was to never – ever – use the Lord's name in vain. It was rumored that some people of indescribable wickedness actually did use God's name "in vain." These sons of the devil attached a four-letter-word as God's last name. But for one Raised Right, this remained a vicious rumor, an urban legend too dreadful to believe. I had never heard such language employed: Until the summer of my twelfth year.

About a half-dozen of my friends and I were playing together on a hot, lazy afternoon. It was the kind of idle summer day that preadolescent boys use to get in trouble, and we did not disappoint. We were playing with a knife. No real explanation beyond that is necessary. I will add only that this huge Rambo-style dagger somehow got airborne. It landed squarely in the center of Michael Holden's right thigh.

He shrieked in pain, "God damn it!!!"

The sun grew dark from the sixth to the ninth hour. The veil of the temple was torn in two. Time stopped. Five twelve-year-old boys slinked off to home without a word. We left Michael sitting there with the knife piercing his Levi's. We knew he would be dead by morning, not from a knife wound mind you, but by the hand of the angel of the Lord, who would strike him down in vengeance for his sacrilege.

I'm not recommending you add this irreverent phrase to your regular vocabulary, but this is not a commandment against cursing, per se. If only it was that easy!

"Thou shalt not take the name of the LORD thy God in vain," means "Don't profess a faith in God with your words – invoking his name – and then betray him with your actions." When we do that, we make his good name, vanity, useless, or worthless. This is not about using the English word "damn" with God's name, as much as we bristle when we hear or use it. It is a commandment against hypocrisy.

God's name is so high and holy we don't even know what it is. Not really. The ancient Hebrews wouldn't even spell it out for fear of defaming him. It was too sacred to even put on paper so the scribes would leave out the vowels, leaving later readers to more or less guess.

The Hebrews understood that when you use God's name as the umbrella over your life, your words, and your actions, be certain that your life, words, and actions, represent him properly. To do otherwise, is to take his name "in vain." It is to defraud him. It is to be a hypocrite. Hypocrisy usually raises its ugly head, not when we pray or in our houses of worship, but in how we speak to and treat others. The words aimed at others – God's creatures – are indirectly aimed at him.

What we say about and to others can either glorify or defame the God we worship. The "sticks and stones," to use the children's rhyme, we throw at our neighbors, are actually being thrown at God. For how we treat others is the clearest testament of how we treat the One we worship.

If only honoring the third commandment was as easy as not saying a particular black-listed word. We'd have it beat. But living and speaking in a way that properly represents our Creator? I guess that's what being Raised Right was all about in the first place.

Ronnie McBrayer

Babushka

Years ago my sister traveled to Eastern Europe, Russia, and the Ukraine on a mission trip. She worked among the indigenous Christians on a number of worthy projects. And when her time ran up, she returned home with a heart full of joy, a head full of memories, and bags full of strange and wonderful souvenirs. Since I'm the only twin brother my sister has, she brought me a unique gift. I got a set of Babushka dolls, those traditional Russian nesting dolls. When you open the first doll it has a smaller doll on the inside, so on and so forth, until you reach a tiny weeble-wobble deep within.

Actually my gift wasn't that special. You can pick up Babushkas for pennies on the rubles. When my sister thought of me she probably thought, "How little can I spend and still appear thoughtful." Whatever. I know how it works. Anyway, this was after Russian *Perestroika*, Polish *Solidarity*, and the other movements that unhinged communism in Eastern Europe. At the time Boris Yeltsin was president of what was left of the Soviet regime.

The outer doll of my Babushka set was, entertainingly, Boris Yeltsin. His likeness had a dopey little smile and rumpled hair as if he had been drinking too much vodka, accurately portrayed I fear. When Yeltsin was opened, there was Gorbachev with the familiar birth mark on his forehead. Inside Gorbachev was Khrushchev, then Josef Stalin, and finally Vladimir Lenin himself. I now keep all these little Communists boxed in the attic. They are much too dangerous to be let loose in the world again.

The deeper you went within the dolls, the closer you got to the essence of Soviet power, its source and beginning. As layer after layer fell away, and finally you held a tiny characterization of Lenin in your hand, you could truthfully say, "Ah, now I've gotten to the bottom of it all. This is the seed, the kernel from which all others grew."

I, and many others, have tried this with Jesus. We all do, I suppose. We have struggled to unravel him, to break open his shell, and then the next, and the next, and the next. We think we can get to the bottom of who he is. We reconstruct his historical setting. We dissect his words. We set out to determine who he "really was" and is. But there is a problem. When dealing with this Jesus, we do not find ourselves moving to something smaller and more manageable. The deeper we go, and as the layers fall away, we move to something greater. He gets larger, more uncontrollable, more inconceivable, more wonderful than our minds can imagine. We are the ones left to weeble and wobble.

Yet, there is a seed, a core to the historical Jesus as well as the exalted Christ of our faith. It is the element of sacrifice. There at the end of it all, when the onion is peeled, is a cross. Jesus, for two millennia, has been marked by this instrument of death. More accurately, he has been marked by the cross since before the threads of time were ever spun. He was "slain before the foundations of the world," John the Revelator said.

There is a cross hanging above my desk where these words are being typed. I wear a crucifix around my neck. I even have a Celtic version of the symbol inked into my skin. And while I behold the cross every day, I cannot take hold of all its implications.

C. S. Lewis challenges us to look at the cross, not as a display of godly anger toward Jesus or the world, but as a Lover absorbing the shame and humiliation of betrayal and unfaithfulness. Lewis said, "Jesus shows on the cross that God's love is not about violence and retaliation. The cross is the only true language of forgiveness."

That stick of wood is a display of agonizing love shown to a world lost in self-centeredness and self-delusion, a world that has done nothing but be disloyal to and reject its Maker. The cross shows us how far Love will go: God, humiliated and bleeding in a suffering mess, bearing up underneath the betrayal of His own creation.

If you can get to the bottom of that, let me know. You're a smarter person than most.

Have A Coke And A Smile!

I struck up a conversation with a man at the coffee shop the other day. He was a nice chap. We talked about the usual neighborly dribble: The weather, the news, work. When he discovered I was a Christian, he could not have been more delighted. He too was a person of deep faith. And my perspective on beliefs and faith became the only topic to which he wanted to speak.

This always makes me feel really weird. It is the reason I am sometimes slow to reveal my vocation. I'm not ashamed of my faith or what I do for a living; not in the least. But Christians are the most fixatedly suspicious people I know. When a Christian discovers that someone else is also a Christian, they always want to square him or her up, to find out what "kind" of Christian he or she is.

Are you a Methodist/Lutheran/Pentecostal or a Liberal/Evangelical/Catholic? What label does this other person wear? And when they find out that someone is of the ministerial persuasion (a reverend, preacher, or super-spiritual-holy-man-or-woman), well, it becomes something like a press conference, as they pepper you with a million theological questions like "Where did Cain get his wife?"

Or, as with my new-found coffee companion, they squeeze you unmercifully into a preconceived, sanctimonious container. As a minister, they assume you spend all your time reading Old

Testament Hebrew, watching *TBN* or the "700 Club," and polishing your halo. They cannot conceive that those of the ministerial guild would actually enjoy drinking a beer and talking about football instead of faith, and that some of us don't like *TBN* or the "700 Club" at all. So I turned the conversation, best I could, to a recent movie I had seen. That was a mistake.

First, it was a movie with an "R" rating, and I was informed that such a transgression did not promote "family values." And second, in the course of our little chat I had revealed that I saw the movie on a Sunday afternoon: On the Lord's Day. Here is where my friend moved from visions of my personal holiness to antagonistic, investigative reporter. My smudged ministerial halo was now slipping off its axis, and he obviously could not understand how this was possible.

In frustration he asked, "What if Jesus had returned while you were in that movie house on the Christian Sabbath; what would you have done if Jesus had walked in and sat down beside you?"

Really, that's not a bad question when you think about it. I suppose if Jesus had actually walked in, I and everyone around me, would have shriveled into the floor like Dorothy's Wicked Witch of the West or John the Disciple on the Island of Patmos. When said John had a mind-numbing vision of the risen Christ he collapsed to the ground as if struck dead.

But since my halo was hanging on by only the tip of a devil's horn, I answered with more sarcasm than sanctity. "Well," I said, "I believe I would have bought him a coke and a large popcorn." Need I say that our conversation ended?

Why is it that Christians seem to be the most uptight people in the world? If someone seems to be enjoying life, this is almost always translated by the Christian establishment as some kind of misbehavior. Where did we get the idea that faith has to be so staid and somber, so legalistic and afraid?

Recently, a friend asked me a weightier question than my hypothetical reaction to Jesus in a movie theater. She asked, "In your work, speaking and writing, what do you hope people will take away from it all?" I'll answer her here: My hope is that people will take spirituality – particularly Christ-centered spirituality – seriously, but not take themselves so seriously. My wish is that people of faith would be exactly that: People of faith. Then, they just might discover the ability to lighten up and live.

Yes, Jesus could show up the next time I find myself in a movie theater. If so, I will probably melt down like so many discarded candy wrappers and popcorn buckets on the floor. But his words to me – his words to us all – would probably be the same he spoke to John on Patmos: "Don't be afraid."

So enjoy the movies and save him a seat.

The Hazards of Gallbladders And Glove Boxes

Pastor Jeff Miller once inspired the congregation at the Seaside Chapel with the retelling of his wife's laparoscopic cholecystectomy. That's swanky medical lingo for "surgery to remove the gallbladder."

Pastor Jeff is quick to tell a tale or two about his wife, recent surgery included. She awoke from her surgery with the immediate sensation that she was better. She had felt so bad for so long she had forgotten what it was like to feel well. Now she felt great! And Jeff compared this relief to finally getting rid of those nagging doubts and worries that just will not go away. It was a memorable parable. Many of us live with so much anxiety that we too have forgotten what it's like to feel well.

So I left church on this particular Sunday thinking about the pesky worries of living; how they are just like a burning in your stomach, an ache in your head, or a nausea that cannot be relieved. Before the day was over, however, I had a bit different metaphor to work with.

Immediately after church my wife and son traveled to the local grocery for a few items to round out Sunday's lunch menu. She called me from Publix in a panic. "I have an emergency!" she screamed into the cell phone.

I admit it, her words unnerved me. To make matters worse, Cindy had not had an award-winning day. Earlier in the morning she had begun her day by crashing my new car into a telephone pole. When I say "new" car I'm not exaggerating. It had not yet been in my possession for twenty-four hours. It was her first moment behind the wheel and before she moved more than ten feet – crash, boom, bah!!! The new car smell must have overwhelmed her senses. She followed this episode with an emergency at the grocery store.

"What now," I thought. Had she fallen on squashed fruit in the produce section, breaking both her legs? Had she lost our four-year old somewhere in frozen food section? Had she run over a bag-boy in the parking lot? In those few seconds I felt my own gallbladder tighten up and wondered briefly what it would take for me to begin to feel well again. But in a million years, with an infinite number of guesses, I would have never anticipated Cindy's emergency: She had discovered a mouse in the glove box of her SUV.

Upon arrival at my wife's rescue I concluded that she had neither hallucinated nor been drinking. There in the glove box, right next to the insurance card and sunglasses, was a nicely crafted mouse nest. The mouse himself had vanished. But the presence of a rodent in her car made the vehicle un-operable of course. There was no way she was getting behind the wheel with a wild animal lose inside somewhere. With a hard gulp I handed my car keys over to her and prayed everyone would get home safe.

Gallbladders, fender benders, rodents in glove boxes: How can things so small cause so much trouble? They wreck your digestive system, stir your irritation, and ignite enough anxiety to keep a team of psychologists busy for a month.

Paul, writing to wearied and worrisome Christians like me, said, "Don't worry about anything; instead, pray about everything. Tell God what you need, and thank him for all he has done."

What is the substitute for worry? Prayer. How do I protect myself from the anxieties that claw at my mind? Let God know how I feel. Where should I go when trying to escape my fears? I should go to my prayer closet. This is the best solution. And when I pray, I shouldn't keep a short list. "Pray about everything," Paul says. That includes your finances; your marriage; your health. Pray about your children's behavior at school; your elevated cholesterol; about having enough homeowners insurance during hurricane season. Pray about your painful gallbladder; your scratched bumper; your rodent invasion. These are not trivial items. For the small worries add up to become substantial angst.

Josh Billings said, "It is the little things that fret and worry us; we can dodge an elephant, but we can't dodge a fly." True. Sometimes we can't even dodge a telephone pole.

Crashing Computers, Crashing Faith

Maybe faith is a lot like your personal computer. Is that a stretch? Well, consider it: No one really thinks about their computer until it stops working. Faith isn't much different.

I spent some time once with a young lady who was convinced God was going to heal her of a serious sickness. She had all the right lines:

"I'm going to pray through to victory."

"God has given me a word of faith."

"By his stripes we are healed."

"I'm just trusting Jesus."

She spoke these words with conviction, over and over like a magical mantra. But I felt she was trying to talk herself into a hoped-for outcome, more than giving testimony to genuine faith. Then, it happened. Not healing, but surgery. She was devastated; and not in the garden variety way of being disillusioned. No, this was a bona fide spiritual crisis. What she believed – her personal faith – was reduced to ashes, consumed in the fires of disappointment.

As instructed by her spiritual leaders, she had, as it were, dutifully shoved coins into the Jesus-shaped vending machine that informed her understanding of God. She got nothing in return. No amount of smashing buttons, shaking heaven, or demanding a refund would change that.

I spoke to her after her surgery and did my best to explain that faith isn't always an escape hatch. That having faith doesn't mean we always avoid trouble, like a cosmic "Get out of Jail Free" card. Instead, as disturbing as it is, faith sometimes leads to troubles. But in the process, faith is the only thing to get us through it. I was met with a cold, empty stare and nary a spoken word. Her faith, at least faith as she had known it, was no longer functional.

Leaving her, I immediately met a friend for lunch at a local Chinese buffet. He arrived red-faced and breathing fire even before we got around to the Hunan chicken. It seems the computer system at his office was on the blink. Ugh. Heaven knows I can commiserate. Can't we all? I have never seen anything make otherwise normal, white-collar, professional people (including myself) go absolutely banshee-bonkers than a malfunctioning computer. Let the computer system crash at the company office, deprive people of their precious e-mail, let everyone know that all hard drives are fried along with everything on them and there will be much more than a crisis.

Formerly mild mannered corporate cogs will be transformed into bloodthirsty hooligans with torches and pitchforks to boot. They will lie in wait outside the IT engineer's office until they have had the opportunity to tear him or her to pieces. So you see, computer crashes and crises of faith have more in common than you

Keeping the Faith

may have realized. When faith and computers work, life is grand. When either of these fail, well, it hits the fan.

As they are similar in failure, maybe they are similar in recovery. Maybe the problem isn't faulty faith or crashing computers at all. Maybe it's a virus. I'm no computer-geek but I know that a computer virus is a nasty piece of work. It so screws up the operating system and the other software on the computer, that actions as simple as sending an e-mail become impossible.

Likewise, many of us have viruses in our faith. Sure we have faith, but there are tiny bits of contamination that have wormed their way deep into our operating system. We may not even know these invaders are there until we call upon our faith to actually work. Like in times of sickness, or when we have marital problems, or in rearing children, or faced with financial crisis, or when we can't access our e-mail. Then, with the pressures of life bearing down upon us, we will find out if our faith is functional.

So what do you do if your faith seems a bit virus weakened? Well, don't throw it all away. That would be akin to chunking your new laptop just because your spreadsheets won't load. Instead, take the time to do a little maintenance. Scan your files. Fix the firewall. Delete the corrupted files. Protect your faith from the glut of enemies it naturally has. Then, reboot, power up, and get to work.

You've got mail waiting in your inbox.

Up The Hill Again...And Again...And Again...

Have you ever heard of a fellow named Sisyphus? I know. His name sounds like a communicable disease or something like that. But in Greek mythology, Sisyphus was a great king and founder of the ancient city of Corinth. In his day he was an entrepreneur of Trump-like proportions. He presided over his territorial and commercial empire with amazing skill. And like any Wall Street tycoon or mega-corporate CEO, he was cagey and innovative, wealthy and creative. His tactics, however, more resembled those of Tony Soprano than Jack Welch.

Sisyphus was a deceptive, murderous, untrustworthy fellow. This was not a man with whom you conducted business with only a handshake. One had better come to the table ready for a fight, or at least protection against getting whacked. If you read the mythologies about Sisyphus you find him so irritating to the gods that they banished him to hell on at least two or three occasions, depending upon who you read. But he was such a wily character he could even negotiate an escape from the underworld – twice. Nevertheless, his trickery finally caught up with him as such things always seem to do. For his many treacherous crimes he was condemned to an eternity of frustratingly hard labor.

His endless assignment was to roll a huge boulder to the top of a hill, taking all of his strength to do so. Then, every time Sisyphus arrived with his rock at the top of the hill, the thing would roll back down to the bottom. Sisyphus would be forced to begin the process all over again. According to the Greeks, he's still struggling with that stone today. In issues of faith many of us lead a Sisyphean existence. We are always pushing that rock up the hill. Proof of our effort is betrayed by words like:

I've got to do better.

I've got to try harder.

I need to give more.

I need to pray longer.

I'm not good enough.

I have to read more Bible verses.

I should go to confession, mass, prayer meeting, or fill in the blank, more often.

Faith becomes a terribly heavy burden to push up the hill. Like Sisyphus eternally pushing his rock, or a hamster on a never ending exercise wheel, we turn liberating grace into a repressive pseudo-holiness that is nothing short of a deathtrap.

How foreign is this concept to the spirituality of Jesus? Matthew 11 frames the contrast best. I love Eugene Peterson's translation of Jesus' anti-Sisyphean words found there: "Are you tired? Worn out? Burned out on religion? Come to me. Get away with me and you'll recover your life. I'll show you how to take a real rest. I won't lay anything heavy or ill-fitting on you."

Quite the disparity, no? Granted, faith and spirituality are not passive. A healthy faith and a vibrant spirituality do not develop spontaneously without some level of decision or intentionality. We have to give these our attention. But too many of us have an overly-inflated sense of personal responsibility. We think that our spiritual journey and growth depends upon all that we can do. Many of us live – or exist rather, we haven't learned to live – with the old Protestant work ethic hanging around our necks like a yoke. Boiled down to bumper sticker mantra we think: "If it's going to be, then it's up to me." That's nothing short of sacrilege, even if it sounds resolute and brave.

We proponents of the Christian faith must recapture a healthy spirituality that isn't so much about labor as it is about resting. It should not be so much about all the work we can do for God, or church, or anyone else. It should be about recovering what it means to be truly alive. Being a follower of Christ is not about being an adherent to one of the world's great religions. God save us from enduring any more of that. No, being a follower of Christ is the discipline of being still, and learning to trust the way that leads to life.

There will always be another stone to push up a hill, another mile to run, another burden to bear. But faith should not be one of these. Faith, particularly faith in the person of Christ, is not a ball-and-chain, holding us down in a slave's hell. It is the very means to live a light and free life.

Keeping the Faith

Ite Missa Est

Churches are peculiar places. I have had the opportunity to serve a few of them. Some of my pastoral experiences have been remarkable and rewarding – baptisms, weddings, the transformation of individuals and families. Some other experiences have been about as much fun as a sharp stick in the eye.

And the churches which I have served have met in a diverse number of places: In the hollow of a school gymnasium; in a leaky storefront on the wrong side of the tracks; in a multi-million dollar sanctuary with all the technological bells and whistles; in an old redbrick church so old it barely escaped the fires of General Sherman's army. In fact, some of the deacons in that old redbrick church may have served in Sherman's army. Speaking of a sharp stick in the eye, they certainly had the attitude and constitution for it. But I digress.

Here is one of the things that make churches peculiar: The most heated arguments in the church were not over our location or theology or future plans. No, the worst controversies I ever endured were over our style of worship.

Should we use hymnals or modern worship music? Should drums be allowed in the sanctuary? Is it blasphemy to move the pulpit to accommodate the children's choir? What would happen if someone clapped or raised their hands during the solo? These are the questions that send the pastor scurrying to his or her gastrologist.

See, with all these exotic locales came an equally exotic variety of worship styles. I've preached after a stately anthem performed by robed choir members and pipe organs. I've tapped my foot and clapped my hands to the cranking riffs of old hippies with electric guitars. I've listened closely to the tight four-part harmony of southern gospel. I've worn a suit and tie to church; and I've worn shorts and sandals.

I've delivered time-honored three point sermons with a poem and a prayer; and I've preached with the technological assistance of projectors and PowerPoint. I've witnessed the traditional Easter cantata; and I've even seen a few interpretive dance steps across the church podium. And all this worship diversity was in a single strain of the Protestant tradition! This doesn't account for the truly wild multiplicity of worship expression that stretches across the Christian sphere from the Pentecostals to the Presbyterians. Praise the Lord and pass the Pepcid.

Which of these styles is "right?" I don't presume to know. Our form of worship will always be dictated by our traditions, our culture, and our context. A look at how Christians from other countries worship proves this point. "Which worship style is right" is, after all, the wrong question. The better question is this: "Does our worship push us out of our church sanctuaries (or wherever it is we meet) to be Christ to the world?" In other words, "What happens when the worship service is over?" This is the more appropriate question.

If our worship moves us past ourselves to the risen and redeeming Christ sent to love the world, then the worship is "right." If our worship sends us into the community as the Father sent his own Son, then it is empowered with spirit and truth. But if our worship focuses us, even in subtle ways, on ourselves, then it is selfishness at best and sacrilege at worst. It isn't worship at all.

The final words of the old Latin mass were, *Ite missa est* – "Get out!" The priests who daily invoked these words over their congregations understood worship's purpose. When the last song is sung, the last prayer offered, and the last homily delivered, the goal of all worship is to redemptively and missionally leave the sanctuary in service to others.

So, take your pick: Sermons or liturgy; southern gospel or rock and roll; drums or pipe organs; corporate prayer or contemplation; kneeling benches or mosh pits. But if these things do not translate into loving action in the community, if these things do not force us out of the building and out to others, we aren't being worshipful at all.

Does worship style matter? Sure it does. But worship substance matters all the more.

Ronnie McBrayer

Unwrapped

Was there ever a time when the holidays were not busy? Probably not. I suppose if we went back to the very first Christmas we would find a great deal of busyness: Joseph was out sitting in the garage on the donkey, honking the saddle horn, doing his best to hurry Mary along just a bit. She was inside packing one more bag for the holiday trip to visit Joseph's neurotic family in Bethlehem.

Of course she was moving as fast as she could. A woman better than eight months pregnant, who was planning an excursion over field and fountain, moor and mountain, was moving no where very quickly. But there were places to go, people to see, and history to be made. So Mary and Joseph hurried on their way into the throngs of people who had gathered in the famed City of David for the census demanded by the Roman authorities.

The story is as familiar as our own children's names. Upon their arrival there was no room for Mary or Joseph at the local Econolodge. So they checked the Fairfield. Strike out. The Motel Six? Nope, not there either. The young couple was forced into being squatters at the local KOA campground. There Jesus was born, ignominiously into a Palestinian backwater. All the while the counting of people, taxes, sheep and profits went on unhindered. The world was too busy to note his arrival.

Keeping the Faith

Last Christmas season was very busy at the hospital where I work. There was a high census of patients. There were extraordinary cases in the Intensive Care Unit and Emergency Department. The entire staff was attempting to coordinate help for patients who would not have a Christmas for their families. In our busyness, we were on the verge of overlooking the old "reason for the season." Then, one of the hospital volunteers, unknown to her, brought me a needed reprieve and put a smile back on my face. She came rushing into the Pastoral Care office with the panicked words, "Jesus is missing!"

At first, I thought someone had taken another crucifix out of one of the hospital rooms when they discharged to go home. It happens more times than you might imagine. As a person packs his or her bags, sometimes Jesus finds himself among the patient's personal belongings. But no worries; the hospital keeps a whole box of Jesuses in a hidden cabinet to replace the stolen ones. I figure if a person needs Jesus enough to steal him off the wall of a Catholic hospital, then by all means, take him.

But the missing Jesus this flustered volunteer spoke of was the baby Jesus from the Nativity scene. Each year in the hospital chapel there is put on display a beautiful, hand carved set of traditional Advent figures. Everyone was there: Mary, Joseph, the magi, shepherds, sheep, donkeys, angels – all the usual suspects. Except for Jesus. The manger was empty.

Our volunteer concluded that he had been stolen, snatched from his crib while sleeping. The Christmas carol says the shepherds were watching and guarding Jesus. Apparently not in the hospital chapel. But it was quickly clarified that Jesus was not missing. He simply hadn't arrived yet.

Baby Jesus was wrapped, not in swaddling clothes, but in shrink wrap and stuck in a drawer. He was safe and sound waiting for Christmas Day before making his grand entrance. We, along with all the Nativity scene characters, wait for him until then.

Advent, that season in which Christians celebrate the arrival of Jesus the Christ, has begun. In your own heart Jesus may be locked away, collecting dust in some dark little corner. You may have grown so busy that you have not even thought of him since last year (or at least since Easter). If so, I think he's do an unwrapping, don't you?

Break the packaging. Knock off the dust. Get him out of the drawer. Let him take his place at the center of this Advent season, and at the center of your life. We may be busy, but not so busy that we forget to "glorify and praise God for all we have heard and seen" in this child born in Bethlehem.

Low Food Or No Food

The United States Department of Agriculture (USDA) issues a hunger report every year. It is a barometer of sorts that gauges Americans' access to food. Their latest report has determined that no one in America is going hungry. Sound like good news? Think again.

Authors of the report have determined that hunger is "not a scientifically accurate term for the specific phenomenon being measured in the survey." The geniuses at the USDA have concluded that hunger is incalculable and the term should be dropped. In other words, there are no hungry Americans. Now, there are thirty-five million Americans who cannot put food on their tables at least part of the year. Of these, eleven million consistently do not get enough to eat.

But they are not hungry. No sir. Don't think that for a minute. This is the twenty-first century and there have been incredible advances in both food production and language. These eleven millions Americans are experiencing, and I quote, "very low food security." But they are not "hungry." That term no longer applies.

"Very low food security?" No, these people are starving. My mother is not "vertically limited." She is short. My children are not "organizationally unprepared," they are messy. My ex-wife was not "monogamously challenged." She was a cheater.

I'm all for politeness and respect but come on. When did it become so hard to tell the truth? Why can't we use words that expose the reality of our world? Why must we play these verbal games of hide and seek? Granted, the truth is hard to face sometimes. Maybe that is why we avoid it with our language. The truth is uncompromising, unrelenting. It will not allow us to make it something it is not. Thus we are forced to speak of it in squishy ways so as not to offend our sensibilities.

Pilate, the Roman governor of Palestine, presided over part of the trial of Jesus. He was a judge; an arbitrator; an evaluator. His mandate was justice. His currency was truthfulness. But facing this man Jesus confused and confounded Pilate. The governor was reduced to indecision, waffling back and forth in his verdict. In the interaction between these two men Jesus said to Pilate, "All who love the truth recognize that what I say is true." Pilate seemed especially rattled by this statement. He pointedly looked into the eyes of the Christ and asked the question we must all face, "What is truth?" But Pilate didn't wait for the answer. Pilate symbolically washed his hands of the whole affair and gave Jesus over to be crucified.

The cold hard truth – in this case the battered, bloody truth was too much to face. It was more convenient to kill the truth than to set it free in the world. Because everyone knows that once the truth gets out, things get messy. If the truth is told Jesus might be found to be innocent. If the truth is told it may be discovered that those who are suppose to uphold justice are actually crooked. If the truth is told we might find hungry Americans just outside our gated well-to-do neighborhoods.

Reverend David Beckmann, who leads the non-profit organization Bread for the World, was rightfully appalled by the latest USDA report on "very low food security." His organization works hard to feed the poorest citizens of the world – including those eleven million hungry Americans. He said, "We should not hide the word 'hunger' in our discussions of this problem because we cannot hide the reality. To do so is a disservice to those who struggle to feed themselves and their families."

Call me "intellectually impaired" or just plain stupid, but I still believe the truth will set us free. It will free us to do what we should do. It will free us to be what we should be. It will free us to face the world for what it really is. It will free us to live a life in service to others. May God help us if we allow decorative words to get in the way of reality.

"What is truth?" I think we know. The real challenge is not defining it, but facing it; and then having the courage to do what we should.

Of Jackrabbits And Jethro

My wife Cindy is a jackrabbit. Do you know what that means? Well, let me clarify. Cindy and I are bike riders. No, not the motorized, belching exhaust type, but the human-powered, pedaling type. We are bicycle riders. She rides a traditional upright road bike and most of the time I ride a laid-back recumbent style bicycle. We have learned that bicycle riding is good for your health and your marriage. There are few sports we enjoy more than ripping off early morning miles before breakfast. We enjoy the exercise and the time together.

Cindy, as I said, is a jackrabbit. "Jackrabbit" is my term for one who jumps off the starting line of her bike ride each morning as if her butt was on fire. Cindy always sets a brisk pace in the coolness and freshness of each day. I admit that when we begin, I can't catch her. It takes a dozen miles or so before my legs and lungs wake up. I spend the first part of our rides together as a dot in her rearview mirror.

This jackrabbit approach to cycling only has one problem: Setting a fast pace and keeping that pace are two very different animals indeed. The jackrabbit of the morning can quickly become the tortoise of the afternoon. So as Cindy disappears over the horizon in the opening miles of the day, I bide my time. I set a steady pace, knowing I will catch up to her down the road. There

Keeping the Faith

she will be, curled up in the fetal position along the side of the road, sucking wind.

Are you a jackrabbit? Are you that type "A" personality? Do you have a gung-ho kind of approach to life with only two speeds, fast and faster? Do you love to grab hold of huge, Herculean tasks and whip them into submission? If so, hey, I tip my hat to you. You get more done before lunch than most people get done in a week. But a word of warning: Will you be around when the day is finished, or will you too be lying in the shade frothing at the mouth and sucking wind?

Remember, this jackrabbit approach to life and work has only one problem: Setting a fast pace and keeping that pace are two very different animals.

The Old Testament patriarch, Moses, led the people of Israel out of Egypt and out of slavery. Bravely he marched into the land of the Pharaohs and demanded, "Let my people go!" Even as I write these words, in my mind I see Charlton Heston, staff in hand, staring down Yul Brynner in the Egyptian sand. Could two actors have looked any more "biblical"?

After the escape from Egypt, the deadly plagues, and the crossing of the Red Sea, Moses' job as deliverer was complete. His role transitioned from acclaimed savior to not-so-glamorous administrator. The people brought all their troubles and disputes to Moses for him to arbitrate. From early in the morning to late at night, day after ceaseless day, Moses was there settling the quarrels of others. He started well, but before long the jackrabbit was exhausted.

Moses' father-in-law, Jethro, came to him with constructive criticism, as father-in-laws are prone to do with the foolish boys who marry their daughters: "This is not good! You're going to wear yourself out," he said. "This job is too heavy a burden for you to handle all by yourself" (See Exodus 18).

Moses' father-in-law went on to tell Moses to share the load. Get some help. Set a manageable pace. Yes, do the important work God has assigned you, but do it in a way you can finish, not just begin.

The one life you have been given to live is not a sprint. It is a marathon. If you use up all your energy today, setting a tempo impossible to maintain, the race will not carry you across the finish line. It will only carry you to an early grave.

You've got a long way to go. Take care of yourself. Stop and rest when you need to. Eat right. Do a little sight-seeing along the way. Let others help you. Pace yourself. Take Jethro's counsel to heart: "You're going to wear yourself out." You may not finish first, but at least you will finish. That's better than lying stupefied in the shade.

Bad Juju

"Be sure your sins will find you out." That's what the Good Book says. My mama said it a lot too. In fact, my mother once arranged for the public display of this proverb. I'm just glad I wasn't on the receiving end of her righteous indignation.

It was during a time in my childhood we now call middle school; seventh grade to be exact. My bagged lunch was kept in my homeroom, and I returned from math class to retrieve it each day. Someone began stealing my lunch on a daily basis. Now, my family was poor. We didn't have a whole heck of a lot. My frugal mother could spread the family budget a bit further by spreading peanut butter on a couple of pieces of bread rather than buying school lunches every day. So the robbery of my lunch was like stealing from my father's meager pay check.

My mother did what you are supposed to do: She complained. Still, the thievery continued. That no one at the school seemed capable of correcting this wrong really sent her five foot, one inch frame into orbit. So, she did something I have rarely witnessed in her since I entered the world. She took matters into her own hands.

This was highly uncharacteristic. Understand, my mother isn't timid, but she is a rule-keeper. A legalist at heart, she plays within the bounds. But not this time. My mother made a sandwich combining dog food and that greasy potted meat compost stuff. Knowing the thief would only get a bite or two of this down, she sweetened the deal with a nicely baked Ex-Lax brownie. The thought of my good Christian mother orchestrating and executing such a devious plan of revenge made my teenage heart leap with joy.

"By God, now we're talking! Enough of this mamsy-pamsy 'turn the other cheek' stuff. Justice will finally roll down like the waters!"

Or at least said justice would be expulsed from every orifice of the offender's body. Either way was fine with me.

On the appointed Day of Judgment I placed my lunch in its usual location and went on to math class. When I returned to fetch my lunch, to my sinister delight, it was gone. I nearly wet my pants with excitement. I watched the absentee roll for the next several days. Dexter Wilkey missed three days in a row and finally returned to school with a peaked and poor look about the eyes. Mother and I had our man. The statute of limitations has expired so I reveal the identity of the bandit here for the first time. Shame on you Dexter.

When I reported this information to my Bible-reading, rule-keeping, daily-praying, no-card-playing, mama, her eyes fired up. She cocked her head back like some twisted marionette and crowed, "Hah! Remember this boy; be sure your sins will find you out!" I reckon they will.

How is it that our wrong-doings always float to the surface? They are like the continual reincarnation of some bad horror movie villain. They just won't go away. They won't stay dead. Cheat on

Keeping the Faith

your taxes and lo and behold that's the one year out of thirty you get audited. Cheat on your wife and that will be the miss-opportune time she decides to investigate the extra charges on your Visa card. Steal from your boss and expect a pink slip. Make purchases you never intend to pay back, and one night the re-po man will be sitting in your driveway.

It might take a while to catch up with you, but catch up is coming nonetheless. Sure, some will get away with it – whatever "it" may be – but there aren't many. Call it sin, or the inescapable justice of the universe, or the law of karma, or bad juju – whatever. "It" has a way of catching up with you like so many persistent bill collectors.

So what is the solution? Wave the white flag of surrender. Stop skimming off the till. Stay faithful to your spouse. Cut up a credit card. Be honest at work. Quit stealing little boys' lunches. It's never too late to do the right thing. Never.

Unless of course you've got that brownie half-way down your throat already. If that's the case, well, Godspeed brave soldier. Your sins have caught up with you after all.

PARABLES

Keeping the Faith

Catch The Wave

When I was a bit younger and a bit braver, a group of friends and I shot the rapids on the Ocoee River in southeast Tennessee. The Ocoee, which I think is the Cherokee word for "terrified rafter" is a world class adventure, so much so that it was the site of the 1996 whitewater Olympic events. Now, I'm no Olympic athlete, and that became evident on the river that day, as I so feared being sucked out of the boat, I literally dug my toenails into the rubber boat I was paddling. By the time we finished, I was on a first name basis with rapids named Broken Nose, Table Saw, and Diamond Splitter. If you're up for a bit of excitement, it's a recommended trip, for fear can be fun.

Whitewater sports began quite accidentally on this mighty river. The Ocoee is dammed in three different places to produce electricity. The Tennessee Valley Authority (TVA) has operated these dams for years. For the longest, TVA's production of electricity killed the river. Only a trickle of water, no more than ankle deep in places, flowed through the gorge. But in the late 1970s a portion of one of their dams broke, sending the full force of the Ocoee through the canyon for the first time in fifty years. Whitewater outfitters and kayakers jumped all over the opportunity.

Even after the dam was repaired, legislation was passed to protect the recreation that had developed on the river. So, for 112 days a year the Ocoee River is "turned on" for kayaking and whitewater enthusiasts. The rest of the year the Ocoee produces electricity. On the morning I arrived at the river there was nothing but rocks.

"How are we going to shoot the rapids when I can rock-jump across the river and never get wet?" I asked my guide. Speaking like a cross between Yoda and some drug-empowered oracle he said, "Sweat it not, dude. The water is coming." He was right. The water was coming. Thirty miles upstream, in the Georgia Mountains, the water had been released. It took a little while to get there, but I watched as the babbling stream turned into the roiling Ocoee River.

The power of those rapids was incredible. You didn't dictate to the river what you were going to do with your little paddle and rubber dinghy. There was no control over the water. That was an illusion – regardless of what some peep-eyed guide might tell you. You went where the water pushed you. Sure, at times you could steer, paddle or even stop, hiding behind a huge rock; but when released over the rapids all you could do was scream, flay at the water, and pray. The power of the water had been unleashed, and we were just along for the ride.

Living out the life of faith is a lot like whitewater rafting. We have our boat and paddle. We are in this boat with our friends on the same journey. What began as a dribble is now an unstoppable flood. We are paddling along best we can, moved by the unleashed

Spirit of God. And sometimes we are more than moved. Sometimes life and faith are not placid escapades of reflection and peace. Instead, the journey of faith becomes a bone-jarring exercise in survival, crashing over the rocks and through the rapids, threatening to drown us.

We are often jostled from the security of our raft, forced to scream out of desperation for a rope or lifeline of rescue. We struggle and fight just to keep our noses above water. We may get the relieved opportunity to list in quiet pools, catching our breath and resting our muscles from time to time. But then, the water will pick up and we are on our way again.

Sure, there are things we can and should do along the way: Pray, hang on, watch out for our friends, and paddle like hell. But ultimately we are riding the wave of God as he does his good will and purpose. His power has been turned on in our lives, and all we have to do is let it take us where it will. All we have to do is hang on.

He Who Must Not Be Named

John Steele was my first principal. Broad-shouldered and tall, he was the kind of man you might see in football pads on Sunday afternoon, not one walking the hallways of an elementary school. To go with his massive frame, he had a thunderous voice and a tight little Zorro-style moustache. Long, curly black locks flowing down his back completed the intimidating package.

Every day on bus duty, standing there on the sidewalk, he looked out across his world like some kind of god straddling Mount Olympus, ready to call down fire from heaven. And to a tiny first grader, he might as well have been a god, because holy smokes could he bring the fire. See, it was rumored, though never truly confirmed nor contradicted, that John Steele possessed in his office an electric paddle.

The story goes that he plugged it into the wall, let it warm up, and then summarily attached it to the seat of your britches. We all knew there was some kind of hellacious torture device behind his office door. What else could squeeze tears and wails from the eyes and mouths of the school's most wayward little boys? But no one spoke openly about the matter. Sort of like those living in Harry Potter's world afraid to say the name of Lord Voldemort, John Steele's paddle was the instrument of punishment too terrifying to be named.

John Steele fit my elementary image and idea of God. In my imagination God was a tall, dark, brooding figure with a deep baritone voice. Twisting the end of his moustache with one hand and twirling his paddle with the other, he watched over his world like an aloof school master on playground duty.

"Don't play too long or too rough." It's sure to draw his irritated attention.

"Don't break the rules." He's liable to break his paddle over your backside.

"And certainly don't enjoy yourself or appear too happy." A smile on your face will be grounds enough for being dragged away for a beating.

Honestly, I don't know who manufactured this idea of God and planted it in my mind. My parents, my own fears, my pastor's sermons: I suppose all of these conspired together to give God this image. It's taken me most of my adult life to shake it off.

But now, I no longer believe that God is a bully. I don't believe God is irrepressibly angry. I don't think God is peering out of heaven waiting to thump us on the head with a big stick. I used to think this way, and worse, but not anymore. The infuriated-mad-as-hell and I'm-not-going-to-take-it-anymore God of my childhood just doesn't match up with the God revealed to us in Jesus the Christ. Here was a man who, yes, could feel the passion and fire of anger. But he never directed this anger at "sinners." No, his ire was reserved, ironically enough, for the arrogance of the clergy, the church crowd, and the religious.

This God revealed to us in Jesus is a gracious, barrier-breaking, party-inviting, sin-forgiving lover of men and women. This God doesn't throw the unrighteous out on their ear. He invites them to the banquet table. This God doesn't lock the door on his broken, prodigal children. He restores their place and dignity in the family. This isn't a God clutching white-knuckled and angrily to a wooden paddle. This is a vulnerable God whose open hands were nailed to a wooden cross.

My image of John Steele was wrong. In adulthood I have found him to be wonderfully normal. He has hobbies, friends, a wife and family (I even baptized his nephew – weird, huh?). And I discovered that he doesn't eat kindergarteners for breakfast, and his paddle was never electrified. Refreshingly, he is someone you would love to have over to watch the game with and have a beer. To get to know my once intimidating principal I only had to get past my fears and suspicions.

All those times he watched over us in the hallways, and the cafeteria, and the playground, his intention was never to punish or harm us. Rather, he had our best interests at heart. He actually loved – and still loves – the children under his care.

In the end that's not so hard to believe about principals or about God.

Keeping the Faith

Addendum: John Steele retired at the end of the 2007-2008 school year after three decades as an educator. Mr. Steele, great is your reward in heaven.

Jump

January 13, 1982, was a cold, snowy day in the nation's capitol. A massive blizzard delayed the travel of commuters trying to get home and air-travelers trying to leave the city. At the height of the storm, Air Florida Flight 90 took off from Washington D.C.'s National Airport. Just seconds in the air, its wings heavy with snow and ice, the plane struck the 14th Street Bridge and plunged into the icy waters of the Potomac River.

The attempted helicopter rescue of the precious few survivors was viewed on the nation's television sets all afternoon. Hundreds of onlookers gathered on the damaged bridge and the snow covered banks of the river to watch as well.

One man was twenty-eight-year-old Lenny Skutnik, a gopher in the Congressional Budget office. Lenny had a simple life with his wife and two young sons. He had never taken a life-saving or first aid course. Making less than $15,000 a year, paying the $325 a month rent was his biggest regular challenge. Yet, when he saw a woman, Priscilla Tirado, blinded by shock and jet fuel, too weak to grasp the rings being lowered by the rescue helicopter, Lenny quickly went from being an observer to a participant in a daring act of courage. He jumped into the freezing water after her, pulling her to shore and to safety.

Later that month President Ronald Reagan seated Lenny Skutnik next to the First Lady as his special guest for the State of the Union address. Lenny was the first ever "ordinary" American to receive such an honor. President Reagan said, "Nothing had picked Lenny out particularly to be a hero, but without hesitation there he was and he saved her life." Skutnik resisted all efforts to make his risky act into something extraordinary. He said, "Nobody else was doing anything. It was the only way...I just did it."

Heroes, spiritual or otherwise, are not those who have special powers, bulging muscles, and colorful costumes. Nothing could be further from the truth. Heroes are simply those who, even in throat-strangling fear, say their prayers and jump into the water. Whether it's the giant-killer David, the law-giver Moses, the beautiful queen Esther, the missionary-traveler Paul, or the errand boy Lenny Skutnik, heroes are just plain normal people. Yet, this is who God chooses to work with and through: Ordinary people called to take extraordinary risks.

Mother Teresa, an ordinary woman in her own right who did extraordinary things, was once asked if she felt proud of all she had accomplished in her life and ministry. She brought up the donkey that Jesus rode into Jerusalem on Palm Sunday as her answer. She said, "When Christ rode the little donkey into Jerusalem and the people were shouting and praising God, do you think the donkey thought the praise was for him?"

There are no superheroes in the ways of God, only those who will trust and obey. Anything that results in a superhuman or extraordinary outcome finds its source in God, not in those who are mere instruments in his hand, conduit through which he works. No, we can't solve every problem. We can't answer every call. We can't singlehandedly do the heavy lifting that will change the world, but we can do what we can do. We can respond in faith, believing that the same God who calls us will grant us the necessary courage to act.

Tim Hansel says, "You can live on bland food so as to avoid an ulcer; drink no tea or coffee or other stimulants, in the name of health; go to bed early and stay away from night life; avoid all controversial subjects…spend money only on necessities…And still you could fall and break your neck in the bathtub, and it will serve you right."

Yes, the water is cold. The dangers are many. The risk is great. But do not be afraid. Place your bets and roll the dice. Jump into the water. You may not think God can use you where you are, but one thing is certain: He can't use you where you are not.

You are where you are because God has brought you to this place. Seize it. Quit waiting for that big moment to come along. This is the moment. God is calling today. Don't let fear keep you on the sidelines.

Color Blind

All sorts of words are used to describe today's families. Traditional, dysfunctional, multi-generational, blended, just to name a few. I suppose that latter category – blended – would describe the little people living under my roof.

Like most families, my wife and I are parents to children who are very different. One is artistic and sensitive with a tender heart. He values his friendships, his Pokémon cards, and his kitten, Speedy. Another is athletic, defiant, and competitive. He is at home on the football field or at the gym, or the fishing pier. And the youngest seems to have been born to entertain. Crank him up and he pops out like a perpetual jack-in-the-box. But these three sons of mine are different in other ways as well. Two of our boys are adopted, "made at the hospital" they would say. The youngest is a definite DNA match, "made in mom's belly." All three are brothers.

Our two oldest children are only six months apart. It has been the equivalent of raising twins, but the two couldn't be more different. Blayze is blond, blue-eyed with freckles, and with his tender heart came tender skin; the kind that requires 50-plus SPF in the Florida sun. Bryce's skin is the color of a well stirred mocha latte, and he has eyes and hair as dark as Appalachian coal.

When Blayze and Bryce were not yet three years of age they began to recognize their differences. The ultimate revelation came first to Blayze as they were once acting out the roles of Woody and

Buz from *Toy Story*, complete with props and costumes. Blayze paused from play to look at his brown cowboy hat. He thought for a moment, then screwed up his mouth and wrinkled his brow. Watching from a distance I knew something weighty was at work.

He crossed the room and laid the well-worn hat against Bryce's skin. Then he laid it against his own bare chest. Back to Bryce, then to himself. Finally, like the apple striking Newton's noggin, he exclaimed in preschool English, "Hey B'wyce! You're b'wown like Woody's hat!" And play resumed without further interruption. It was a realization that simple and that profound.

Blayze and Bryce are now in the second grade. Almost daily they are forced to explain to someone that yes, they are in fact brothers, despite their different appearances. But aren't we all brothers and sisters?

The Apostle Paul wrote, "There is neither Jew nor Greek, slave nor free, male nor female, for you are all one in Christ Jesus" (Galatians 3:28 NIV).

Paul wrote those words nearly two millennia ago, and we are still trying to learn the truth of what he said. Separations of race, religion, culture, ethnicity, and gender have been trumped by the invitation to become one in Christ. His life, death, and resurrection reconstituted and rearranged the world. Again, to quote Paul, he said, "The old has gone, the new has come" (2 Corinthians 5:17 NIV).

Keeping the Faith

God is making all things new, and he has begun with me and you. If we allow him to renew our hearts, to give us hearts like children, we will be enabled to take people as they are, to see beyond color and creed, and join in brotherhood with others, even those very different than ourselves.

Our world has serious problems. I'm not so naïve that I don't recognize this fact. Nor do I think that chummy stories about my own children are enough to solve these problems. Still, it is a start. What would change in our world if the truth about God's family was allowed to prevail? If "all politics if local," as the late speaker of the house Tip O'Neal often said, maybe love works the same way. If I can learn to love those closest to me: On my street, in my neighborhood, under my roof, then maybe I can learn to love everyone.

With practice I might even learn what it is like to become part of the beautiful, blended family of God.

Ronnie McBrayer

Spinning My Wheels

When my wife insisted that I accompany her to the gym I thought it was a good idea. She had been pressing me about it for some time. And combined with my recent cholesterol readings I finally relented and agreed to go. When she informed me that we must rise at 4:30 in the morning, I hesitated only a moment. I quickly regained my composure to face the challenge. When she told me we would be participating in a cardiac spinning class I didn't even blink. I've spent hours – literally days at a time – on a bicycle with a couple of hundred mile rides in my repertoire.

"Spinning class? Why didn't you say that's where we were going? No problem."

This would be a cinch. I strolled into the gym in my cycling shorts with enough bravado to take the lead in a John Wayne flick.

The class was led by a lean, hard, athletic woman with the body fat of a celery stick. She seemed harmless enough. She warmly introduced herself and set me up on my bike. She made small talk with others about work and children. Then the class started and everything changed. Celery girl turned into a whirling tormenter. She began and kept a pace that Lance Armstrong would have cringed at. She barked orders. She coached and screamed out encouragement. I screamed too. In agony. Oh I kept up appearances for a while. My pride would let me do no other. I mean, my wife was in the room. Sure, we've been married a while and she knows who and what I am. But still, I wanted to prove this old man still had a little left in the tank.

Ultimately, however, I was reduced to a sweaty, light-headed heap with what felt like coal burning in my lungs. The instructor and her little group of cycling fascists, including my wife, disappeared over the spinning horizon. I was in over my head. I finally admitted it.

The night before my cardiac adventure I had read the accounts of Simon Peter's denial of Jesus. You may remember the story. Simon Peter, full of bluster, made bold promises about his commitment and abilities in the face of adversity.

"Suffering on cross? Why didn't you say that's where we were going? No problem."

This would be a cinch as Simon boasted that he would go to the wall – to the death if necessary – in his commitment to Christ. Even if everyone else fell by the wayside, not him.

"I will never deny you," he said to Jesus.

Jesus, lovingly but uncompromising, told Peter the truth: "Before the rooster crows (even before sunrise and the day begins!) you will deny that you even know me, three times."

Simon Peter was insulted by this lack of confidence. But, by the time the sun rose on what we now call Good Friday, Peter had been reduced to a whimpering defector. Confronted by those accusing him of being a follower of the now arrested and condemned Rabbi, Peter called down curses from heaven. He renounced the Christ he loved and abandoned Jesus to the civil and religious authorities. The outspoken leader of the band of disciples was a turncoat. He was in over his head. Finally, he had to admit it.

Thankfully, Jesus didn't leave him there. After his crucifixion and resurrection, Jesus specifically sought out Simon Peter. Jesus embraced him. Forgave him. Restored him. The shame and self-disgust were washed away by mercy. Simon Peter was a changed man. Yes, he remained gruff and curt; after all he was a hard working fisherman. But he never recovered from the forgiveness extended by the very one he had thrice denied. It ruined him in the best possible way.

We all fail. We all disappoint. We all have our moments – sometimes multiple moments – when the crowd peddles by us. And we sit there exhausted, used up, in over our heads. In those moments Christ comes to us. Not with criticism, but encouragement. Lovingly, he lets us catch our breath. Then, uncompromising, he puts us back on the seat, back in the saddle.

No one who has ever failed, at faith or at riding a bike, has ever gotten fit by lying where they fell.

Sancta Ignorantia

Having lunch with friends recently, we began talking about our earliest childhood memories. Maybe you have a firmer grip on your memory than we do, but none of us could recall anything but flashbulb moments before our kindergarten years. My friends have a young son, not yet three-years-old. He was sitting at the table with us, now throwing French fries across the room. As we talked, his mother looked over at him, turned to the rest of us at the table and said, "If something happened to me now, while he is so young, he would have no memory of me at all."

This sort of threw a wet blanket on our otherwise happy lunch date, but she was right. Here was a child so devoted to and dependant upon his mother that he can never be more than a few feet from her presence, and yet should she vanish, he would not remember her. That observation really got me thinking. Does a child – any young child or baby in arms – really know his mother? No, not in the least; not at all.

He doesn't know his mother's hometown; that she was a cheerleader in high school; that she graduated from college at the top of her class; that she has a remarkable career. He doesn't even know the color of her eyes. He knows nothing of her family history, her most life-shaping experiences, her favorite meal, or how she likes to spend her quiet time – when she gets any quiet time. He knows none of these things. He doesn't know her.

And yet, he does know her, better than anyone else. He recognizes her voice, her laugh, her touch, her smell. Even as a toddler, he could pick her out of room of hundreds of other parents. He loves her, runs after, and cries for her. At the same time, he is both in ignorance of the very one who gave him life, and clings to her with such attachment that he cannot live without her. It is a beautiful *sancta ignorantia* – holy ignorance.

We all live in holy ignorance, even when we are "certain" about the things we believe. Just as a mother makes herself known to her child, God has made himself known to us through his creation, his Scriptures, and supremely though Jesus Christ. We get it; at least enough of it for faith to be born and to grow. But we don't understand it all. We can't. Paul recognized this when he prayed for the Ephesians, "May you have the power to understand, as all God's people should, how wide, how long, how high, and how deep Christ's love is. May you experience the love of Christ, though it is too great to understand fully."

When we speak of Christ we are speaking only of our understanding about and experiences with him. He remains out of our reach. Yes, we know Jesus, but we don't know him, and we will not know him completely this side of the kingdom of God. This doesn't weaken our faith. It pushes our faith forward. We press on in pursuit of more, because the faith we hold on to is incomplete. Our conclusions about God, about Jesus, about the Bible, about our own spiritual experiences, are always unfinished. Yes, we cling with confidence to our faith, and yet we learn to hold to our conclusions loosely.

"Here we stand. We can do no other," as Luther said, and still we know our beliefs will continue to develop over the course of our lifetimes. We confess, "This is what we believe," and yet what we believe is in process.

Faith in Christ is not something we master in this lifetime, no more than completely knowing another person is possible in this lifetime. But our inability to grasp the totality of Jesus Christ is not reason to give up on faith. This does not stop us from loving him, from pursuing him, or from crying after him. It intensifies our chase. For we recognize that the only way to know the unknowable God is to pursue him until he makes Christ "all and in all."

So, the answer to the question of the tent-meeting revivalist, "Do you know Jesus?" is an absolute and positive, "Yes!" followed by an absolute and positive "No!"

Sancta ignorantia: I plead holy ignorance.

If Only Speedy Had Been More...Speedy

My four-year-old son, Braden, has been asking me questions about Speedy. He is particularly interested when Speedy is coming home. Speedy, blessed be his name and God rest his soul, was our pet kitten. He went to be with Jesus last year.

I will not burden you with the details of his unfortunate demise. Let me just say that he was inappropriately named. Had he lived up to the namesake attached to him by my children, Speedy might still be with us today.

Having faced death innumerable times with grieving families, I have learned that it is best not to avoid the Reaper. So, our family had a memorial service for Speedy in the backyard. It was a sad event.

I laid him to rest in a small shoe box, in a hole dug at the edge of the woods. All three of our boys gave eulogies of sorts. My wife was there, in terrible grief (unknown to our children she was the one responsible for Speedy's untimely death); and I said a few prayers. After placing flowers on the grave we went inside for ice cream. There's no sadness a little Neapolitan won't make a little better. And there around the kitchen table, to a preschooler and two third-graders, I explained best I could about the after-life.

I didn't do too good of a job. Because now, months later, Braden has all these questions. They machine-gun out of his mouth like ricocheting bullets.

Braden asks, "When is Speedy coming back?"

I respond, "Jesus will bring him back one day."

"Where is Speedy now?" Braden asks.

"He's in heaven, with Jesus," I say.

"I thought he was in the shoe box under the dirt?" Braden so literally remembers.

And then the bullets really start to fly:

"Am I going to die?"

"When I die will you put me in a shoe box? I don't think I will fit."

"Will I be able to see if you put dirt on my head?"

"How will I open my eyes in heaven with dirt on me?"

"Will you and mom die? I don't want you and mom to die – Who will cook my food for me."

On and on it goes.

I have little letters after my name that mean I spent some time in a classroom learning theology. These letters are supposed to mean I know something about God. Speak for very long with a cross-examining four-year-old, and you learn you don't know squat, letters or no.

Granted, death is a mystery. We pastoral-types don't know as much about dying as we let on. But I suppose death is no greater a mystery than life. We don't know as much about living as we let on either. Yet, on this weekend, we celebrate both: Life and death. We celebrate the macabre crucifixion of our Lord, Jesus, who died on a cross on the paradoxically named Good Friday. And we celebrate his resurrection on Easter Sunday morning, his retaking of his life.

"He is risen," the angel said on that morning so many centuries ago. "He is risen indeed," has been the response from believers, questioners, skeptics, and doubters ever since. Believers echo the traditional response because, well, they believe. The questioners and the skeptics and the doubters whisper those words in return because they *want* to believe. They want to believe that there is a life beyond this one. They want to believe that existence continues beyond the grave. They want to believe that Jesus truly is what the New Testament calls the "first fruits" of the living. That Christ, in rising from the dead, is signaling that he will bring all of God's creation back to life.

I don't pretend to have all the answers. I don't have to unravel every tangled ball of doubt about the resurrection and the hereafter. I don't have to be able to explain it all in neat little charts and precise diagrams complete with scriptural references. I have the risen Christ alive in my heart. That is enough; for he will roll away the stone of disbelief and uncertainty. He will empty the grave of its terror and dread. He will set aside shoe boxes for the purpose of only holding shoes.

And when he comes, he will answer all the questions of little boys and their fathers.

He is risen. He is risen indeed.

Red, Red Wine

James Patterson was a grouchy, opinionated old man. A bad tempered porcupine, always jabbing and needling those around him. He had definite conclusions about life, faith, and politics. We rarely agreed. But he was my friend and I loved him.

One Wednesday evening after church he said, "Come on over to the house, Preacher. I want to give you some corn and 'maters." I tried to pawn him off. I didn't want any vegetables. I wanted to go home. Except James Patterson was not one to be disregarded. He was insistent and I finally complied. He and his wife had lived in the same old farm house for years. They enjoyed their garden, their bird and squirrel feeders, and the red brick Baptist church they had always called home. I would learn on this particular evening that James enjoyed a few more things.

After loading me up with all the sweet corn, tomatoes, and green beans I could carry, James invited me around to the back porch. He shifted and squirmed like a man conflicted. Some inner debate was taking place, a deliberation. I could tell James had something to say or confess. In the twilight moments of the day he was deciding if I could be trusted with his secret. Finally, with a quick bob of his head he whispered, "Come with me."

We walked off the porch to an old storm shelter dug out of the hillside. James fumbled with his keys and no less than four locks on the door. When the door was opened I beheld a magnificent winery.

It appeared that James had been making homemade muscadine and blackberry wine for more than a decade.

He proudly walked me through the process: Decanters, mason jars, plastic tubing. He said, "Jesus turned water into wine. I'm just trying to make as good a wine as Jesus made." James was doing a pretty good job of it. After the tour, James grew solemn. "I know there are a lot of folks down at the church who say they don't believe in this sort of thing. Teetotalers. That's a lie. Everyone of 'em's been down here at one time or another beggin' for a bottle. Hypocrites."

I suggested that we bring it all out in the open. "Tell you what, James," I said. "Let's get rid of the Welch's and substitute some of your brew in the communion cup this Sunday!" James was scandalized. "Lord no, Preacher! We can't do that! What would people say?" With a wink I asked him, "Who's being a hypocrite now?"

The ancient Greeks coined the word, hypocrite. The word was once only a description of the play-actors in a drama troop. When short of talent it was common for an actor or actress to portray multiple characters, exchanging masks when the script called for it. A hypocrite was an actor; a role player; one who wore multiple masks. We are all hypocrites to some degree. The face we show our boss is not the one we show our spouse. The person people see at the PTO meeting is not the person they see at our child's Little League game. This is due largely to the fact that we are multi-

Keeping the Faith

faceted people forced to interact in diverse situations. It's hypocrisy in the original, positive sense of the word. We simply play the role required.

At other times, however, the masks we wear are more sinister. Sometimes we help others, not so much because they have needs, but because we want to be recognized. We condemn others for their shortcomings but stumble around with the proverbial plank in our own eye. We fret and object over violations of the letter of the law, but neglect the weightier issues of compassion, mercy, and justice.

With every inconsistent act we slip on a disguise worthy of a Mardi Gras Day parade. Finally, there comes a point when we not only fail to recognize the duplicity of our actions, we no longer recognize our own face.

James and I never did try to get his wine into the communion service. But we did bring his brewery out of the darkness. Not everyone was happy, of course, but at least those who imbibed were happy to get a bottle of the Patterson Select without hiding it from each other, or the preacher.

Ronnie McBrayer

This Is Just Like Church

I pulled from my mailbox that little envelope that I knew would ultimately arrive: A summons requiring my presence in the halls of justice. Jury duty. So I prepared myself to look as disrespectful as possible; not as a difficult a job as you might imagine. Ratty blue jeans, worn sneakers, an unshaven face and the gaudiest Hawaiian shirt from my closet – this was my effort to appear unmannerly enough to stay out of a week-long trial.

I arrived at the courthouse, got my juror number, took my seat, and watched my peers arrive. I was not the only one less than thrilled about being there. As the seats around me filled, there was more complaining than you would hear on a Better Business Bureau hotline.

One lady in particular charged into the courtroom with defiant words to the bailiff. "I don't want to be here. I'm not happy about this one bit," she huffed. Firmly, the bailiff showed her to her seat. As she trudged by and plunked down in her assigned seat I heard her say, "Oh, this is just like church."

Sitting there I concluded that jury duty was in fact, a lot like church. We were gathered in a small room, compelled against our will, sitting on hard pews when we would rather be doing something else. Further, a man dressed in a long dark robe with a big book sat in magisterial supremacy over us all. He dictated our rising and sitting as if we were androids. You had to have his permission to even visit the bathroom. And no one would be excused unless it was under the direst of circumstances. Heck, this was just like church.

Reading Eugene Peterson recently, he reminded me of the story of Procrustes, an ancient Greek innkeeper. His "inn" was more like a present-day bed and breakfast – his personal home where he entertained sojourners on their travels. Most days he was observed sitting outside his immaculately cleaned home, smoking his pipe, and harmlessly smiling behind a gray beard and kind eyes. But old Procrustes had definite ideas about Greek life and beauty. He had a bed in his home that he claimed would miraculously fit the frame of whoever slept in it and transform them into the perfect Greek.

Many a traveler accepted the offer of this unique bed. Procrustes would then sinisterly enter the room after his guest was sound asleep, and complete the fitting. A short person would be stretched on a rack until he filled the bed. A tall person would have whatever portion of his arms and legs that hung over the mattress sawed off. When the visitor left the next morning, if able, either by extension or amputation, he was now the dimensions of a perfect, beautiful Greek. Of course Procrustes was the one who established the definition of perfection.

What the mythical Procrustes accomplished for a few of his unfortunate fellow Greeks, the church often accomplishes for many of its members. Like some kind of spiritualized McDonalds, many of today's churches turn out carbon-copied, unconscious, "Christians" like hamburgers and fries rolling off a conveyor belt. All must read the same translation of the Bible. All must share the same interpretation and confession with no room for divergent belief. All must have the same social habits and vote in the same political block. Gone is any sense of creativity. Gone is the stretching of the mind and emotions that come from heart-felt disagreement. Gone is the richness of diversity. Gone is the beautiful collage that is the people of God. It is replaced by a monolithic, black and white snapshot.

Take your number. Sit in your assigned seat. Stand when commanded. Dress like the rest. Stay with the herd. It's no wonder some people won't go to church – it's because they have been. It may be hard for us Christian-folks to accept, but the institutional church is often the largest single obstacle to others experiencing Christ. What was once viewed as a doorway to the Divine can quickly devolve into a stumbling block.

So we must ask ourselves: Will we squeeze those around us into Procrustes' bed, doing great damage in the process? Or will we give enough room for people to become who God is making them?

I hope we'll choose the latter.

Please Talk To Me!

One Wednesday afternoon my twin sister and I were ripping up terra firma in my grandmother's fallow garden. We were only five-years-old, just months before beginning kindergarten. My sister, in her clod-crushing zeal, miscalculated the distance between herself and me. I was summarily thumped on the head with a garden hoe.

Two distinct memories fill my mind about that moment: First, the warm, oozing of blood running into my left ear; and second, the sight of my Medicare-receiving, apron-wearing grandmother running, yes, running, from the house to scoop me into her arms.

There were no ambulances in my hometown. There was no real emergency room. There was no 911 service. Even if these things had been readily available, it wouldn't have mattered on this afternoon. My grandmother didn't own a phone or drive a car. My aunt, who lived next door, called my mother at work. She and my father arrived in record time and sped me to the office of Dr. Jerry Barron, one of only three doctors in town.

Dr. Barron was a community acknowledged quack. "I wouldn't let him work on my dog," was a phrase I had heard my entire life. But on this afternoon he was the only option. See, Dr. Thompson did not work on Wednesdays, and nobody really visited Doc Hill anymore, not unless it was an extreme emergency. Doc Hill was very old, and besides that, young mothers had lost all confidence in him. A few years previous he had reported to his clinic early one morning to deliver a new born baby boy, drunk as the proverbial skunk. The delivery was without complication, but the subsequent circumcision was a disaster. Ouch.

So, it was with great trepidation that I was passed with a gushing head wound into the hands and care of Dr. Barron, this silver-haired idiot. I was dragged to an examination room where Dr. Barron separated me from my parents, asking them to remain in his clinic lobby. He, his two nurses and an office receptionist, held me down to place a half-dozen stitches in my scalp. I twisted and turned, convulsed and screamed, begging someone, anyone, to explain what was happening. They continued their work, never saying a word. Finally, I screamed at the top of my lungs, "Will someone please talk to me!"

Apparently that was the magic phrase. Dr. Barron and his team of tormentors actually stopped what they were doing. He looked me in the eyes, explained what they were trying to do, how long it would take, how much it would hurt, and the hoped for result when he finished. I then lay perfectly still, the doctor only moving my head occasionally, until the procedure was complete. I only needed a little conversation and explanation. I just needed someone to listen to me.

Listening is largely a lost art. Medical professionals run us through their offices like cattle through a chute. Politicians stubbornly ignore our voices. Our children discount our counsel.

Our spouses cannot recall the conversation we had just this morning. Heck, even the kid at the fast-food restaurant can't listen long enough to get our order right! As I get older I understand more and more why Jesus often said, "He who has ears let him hear," before uttering some mind-blowing instruction. Because for the most part, we do not use those two fleshy instruments attached to the side of head.

At no time in human history has there been more opportunity to communicate. Land lines, cell phones, e-mail, faxes: We've come a long way from beating drums and smoke signals. Still, most of our advances have been on the speaking side, rather than the listening side.

I wonder what would happen in our homes, in our office cubicles, in the classroom, in the doctor's office, in our church sanctuaries, in the houses of legislation if we who have ears took the time to actually use them.

We just might begin to appreciate, rather than vilify, those on the other side of the aisle. We just might find that the world would grow a little quieter, a bit more peaceful. We just might find that those we have long ignored actually have something worth saying. We just might discover the greatest advancement in the history of human communication – the ability to not say a single word.

Ronnie McBrayer

Take A Mulligan

Years ago, when I served as a pastor in North Georgia, I had an afternoon off. I decided to squeeze in a quick round of golf. There is a suspicion that pastors only work one day a week, so they can golf any time they like. Not so. The "one-day-a-week" work schedule is a vicious rumor propagated by the internet. This was a splendid summer afternoon begging for long drives and birdie putts. So I headed off to the links.

Upon my arrival I was greeted by three guys needing one more to complete their foursome. I jumped in with them and headed for the first tee. The fellow sharing the cart with me was a big, burley gentleman, though gentleman is too complimentary a term. I quickly learned that he had a terrible slice. He put his tee shot into the woods. This ball was chased by two quick mulligans. Upon leaving the fairway vacant, he tore loose with a flurry of colorful language. The adjectives and verbs rolled for what seemed like five minutes.

A knot began forming in my stomach. Cursing doesn't bother me too much. Growing up in the country I learned that farming animals and diesel engines only work when properly tongue lashed with a heavy dose of profanity. The nausea in my stomach was not the result of his vivid use of the King's English. No, it was because I knew at some point in this round, out of innocent socializing, someone in my foursome would turn to me and ask, "So, what do you do for a living?" Things might get a little uncomfortable at that juncture.

I didn't have long to wait.

My cart-partner, upon catching his breath, turned, looked straight at me and said, "I hope to God you ain't no damn preacher."

For a moment the sun slipped behind a cloud and the birds stopped singing. I grimaced and said, "You know, I'm afraid I am." My golf partners just stared at me, eyes bulging from their sockets You can't make this stuff up.

The silence was broken with a stuttering, "You're kidding, right?" To which I said, "I wish I was."

I went on to have one of the best rounds of my life. The other three didn't play very well, not knowing whether to smoke their beer or drink their pot. It was absolutely priceless.

The Psalmist David once prayed, "May the words of my mouth and the meditation of my heart be pleasing to you, O Lord, my rock and my redeemer" (Psalm 19). David rightly understood that the heart and mouth are connected. What is inside a person – in their heart – will eventually be made evident by the words on his or her lips.

I like to think of the heart as a sponge. No, not that muscle in the center of our chest that pumps blood to our extremities. By heart I mean something more Eastern, more Hebrew. The ancient Jews often spoke of the heart as the location of human emotions, passions, and personality. The heart holds, like a sponge, what and who we really are.

When pressure is applied, what is on the inside will come out. There's no stopping it. A driver cuts us off on the highway; our boss questions the quality of our work; our spouse throws barbed words in our direction; an errant tee shot misses the fairway – these act like the wringing and squeezing of our hearts. Such moments can be more than embarrassing. They can be downright hurtful for those around us. For once words are spoken they can never be retrieved or cancelled. These words go on to burn in the ears of those who hear them for a lifetime.

Is it any wonder David prayed that his words, at first born in the quietness of his heart, would be pleasing to God? The only remedy for a mouth run amok is a sanitized heart. If what we say under pressure is going to change, it will be because what is inside us – who we really are – has changed.

When the meditations of our hearts are healthy and clean, so will be the words of our mouths. This isn't a bad idea. You just never know who might be listening.

Keeping the Faith

This Is Going To Be Good

The first Sunday of October is World Communion Sunday. It is an annual event in which Christians worldwide celebrate our oneness in Christ, in spite of our many differences and traditions. Special services will be held throughout the world with the Lord's Supper, the Eucharist, or Communion forming the centerpiece of the worship.

Where I go to church, we observe the Lord's Supper every week. A beautiful lady named Nancy McConnell and her wonderful team always has the elements ready and prepared to serve. It is such a nice change for me to take the bread and cup each Sunday. Because in the Baptist church of my childhood, the Lord's Supper was never weekly; we might have appeared to be Catholic, God forbid.

No, we took Communion quarterly, and typically we observed the ceremony at the end of a Sunday night service. We had those stale little wafers half the size of a postage stamp, and lukewarm grape juice – never wine – in tiny plastic cups. Rarely was this ritual ever explained and never was it central to our worship. It was tacked on as an amendment, an afterthought, on a school night when folks seemed to rush through the motions to get home as soon as possible. I was always grateful for Communion. It meant the sermon was going to be shorter. Hallelujah!

Whether we come to the Lord's Table each day, each week, or once a year, it's how we come to the table that is more important.

We must be careful in the familiar not to lose the wonder and sensation that Christ sits at the table and gives himself for his people as we take the bread and cup. I was reminded of this not long ago.

I attended Christ the King Episcopal Church in Santa Rosa Beach, Florida where Reverend Doctor Frank Cooper serves as the minister. It was a wonderful experience of sights, sounds, and beautifully orchestrated liturgy. And it was unlike anything of my own Christian tradition. Sure, I attend the occasional Catholic mass on a holy day, and I have sat in the pew at many a Catholic funeral. I have participated often in ecumenical services. But to attend a Sunday morning Episcopal mass was new, confusing, and strangely magnificent.

I was amazed at the small children there who were far better acclimated to their surrounding than this free-group intruder. I sluggishly stood, always a few seconds behind the crowd. I found myself standing alone, dropping to the pew after everyone else took their seat. I fumbled with the Book of Prayer and the hymnal, never able to find the readings or the songs on time. By the time for the homily I was a nervous wreck wishing I had read *Episcopalianism for Dummies* before darkening the door.

Father Cooper, well prepared and impressive in his robe, delivered his talk without notes and with the grace developed over decades of sermon delivery. He spoke of sin as "a pre-existing condition" comparing it to his recent struggles with his health insurance. It was wonderful. After the homily, and a number of other confusions for this Baptist-raised child, the invitation was offered to receive Holy Communion. Finally something I understood! I waited eagerly until it was time to go forward, kneel at the altar, and have the elements placed in my hands.

Beside me at the altar was a young family: A dad, a mom, and their three small children. The youngest was probably four or five-years-old. He stood right beside me at the rail, too short to kneel. I looked at him and smiled. He smiled in return, trembling with expectation.

He wiped his wet lips with the back of his tiny hand and coarsely whispered, in a voice that could have been heard at the back of the sanctuary, "This is going to be good!" And it was.

The Wheels On The Bus

We knew this day would arrive. It has been looming on the horizon for years. Some days we prayed it would hurry to us. We anticipated it as eagerly as hungry children eyeing a cookie jar. But most of the time we dreaded it like the plague: Our baby boy has begun school.

Braden McBrayer, all of his five years and forty pounds has slipped the surly bonds of home and his mother's apron strings. He is no longer a "preschooler." School is now in session.

Now, this isn't our first rodeo. He is the third backpack-bearing, lunchbox-toting McBrayer boy to climb onto the big yellow school bus. But barring an Immaculate Conception of some sort, he will be the last to begin this journey.

When I began school so many years ago, I wept. I begged for a reprieve. I clung to my mother's legs and had to be pried off of her and onto the bus. Braden, however, leapt aboard with not even a hint of angst.

As I walked away from the bus stop I thought about how different our two school starts were. I mean, Braden and I are a lot a like. Any one who has ever seen us standing together could never deny that. But the biggest difference between father and son, besides my apparent cowardice, is Braden has big brothers. When I climbed onto the school bus headed for Red Bud Elementary School more than thirty years ago, I was the first in my family to do so.

Sure, I had a twin sister with me that day, but she was almost as afraid as I was; almost – no one was as scared as me.

But Braden has been trying to get on the school bus for more than two years now. Why? Because he wanted to follow his brothers. With those brothers to show him the way, he has no fear, only anticipation. His first day of school was not a shove into the unknown, alone. He has someone who has gone before him.

As a Christian, I am glad Jesus is my Savior. Of course, by using the word "Savior," I mean a lot of different things. He saves from sin and failure. He saves from fear and death. He saves us, yes, even from ourselves. I am grateful for this. I am thankful that the Christian faith plants hope in our hearts, a hope that something lies beyond this world. We believe the afterlife, as much as we do not know about it, is a life with the risen Christ. In short, we believe in a final resurrection. For this, I am glad. But Jesus is also my guide for living today, in the here and now.

To follow Jesus is not just to walk over the horizon of death into the sweet by and by, holding his hand singing "Kum Ba Yah." To follow Jesus today is to, well, follow him. It is to imitate him, to be like him, to take his ways and words to heart, and live by them. The way of Christ is the way of loving our enemies. He teaches us to do good to those who don't deserve it. He challenges us to give away our fortunes and the things we hold dear. He says, "Turn the other cheek." He calls us to take the path toward sacrifice and crucifixion that we too might arise from the dead.

To follow Jesus, if I can be so simplistic, is not unlike a kid brother following in the steps of one who has gone before him. Every day I rise I do so, not thinking about some future "graduation" date from this world. I get up, get dressed, grab my backpack and lunchbox, and follow Jesus into the school of life.

He knows which seats on the bus I should stay away from. He points toward and warns me of compromising situations to avoid. He shows me how to keep my milk money safe and with whom I should share it. He's an old hand at how things work. Jesus, as our way, knows and shows us the ropes. He teaches us how to live, how to love, how to trust, and even how to die.

This takes more than a little fear out of living, for we never have to face the world alone.

Keeping the Faith

All You Can Do Is All You Can Do

In his book, *The Fall of Fortresses*, Elmer Bendiner describes a bombing run over the German city of Kassel during World War Two. His B-17 Bomber was barraged by flak from Nazi antiaircraft guns. That was not unusual. Routinely, if the word "routine" could be used to describe such harrowing feats, Allied planes were riddled with bullets and shrapnel. But on this particular occasion the fuel tanks were hit. Remarkably there was no explosion. This was more than miraculous good fortune.

On the morning following the raid, the crew asked the ground mechanics for the unexploded shell as a souvenir of their unbelievable luck. The crew chief told them that not just one shell had been pulled from the tanks. Eleven unexploded cartridges had been retrieved. Only one would have been sufficient enough to blast the plane from the sky.

So, the persistent, now even luckier crew, went to the armory to find the malfunctioned shells. There they discovered that Allied Intelligence had taken possession of them. There was no reason why at the time, but eventually the crew got the answer. When the technicians at the armory opened each of the defective shells to defuse them, they found no explosive charge. They were empty, harmless, only blank casings.

Except for one; this one contained a carefully rolled piece of paper, no bigger than a cigarette. On it was a scribble of Czech. The

Intelligence officers finally found an airman who could translate the text. Astonishingly it read, "This is all we can do for you now."

At great risk, a Czech worker, under forced labor by the Nazi government was rolling powder-less shells off the munitions assembly line. He was doing all he could for the liberation of Europe, and saving Allied lives in the process. Bendiner and his crew were forever grateful.

A woman once came to Jesus bearing an expensive bottle of perfume. It was worth maybe a year's salary. She broke it open and poured it out on Jesus. This was nothing short of a scandal. This was a woman of ill repute, first of all. And to the witnesses in the room it was a wasteful, irresponsible performance, but Jesus saw the real value of her act. This was an act of worship; a sacrifice driven by her devotion to Christ. Knowing his death was imminent, she was anointing him in advance for burial. That may sound morbid, but Jesus was moved.

He said, over the muttering crowd of onlookers thinking her foolish, "Leave her alone. She has done what she could. This act of worship will never be forgotten." Fulfilling Jesus' words, we've been telling her story now for two millennia.

Little things seem to matter most in Jesus' scheme of things: A young boy with just a few scraps of bread and a can of sardines; an old widow woman with only a penny to drop in the offering plate; someone with faith barely the size of a jelly bean; a prostitute with a bottle of perfume.

Keeping the Faith

Most of us, in our days of glorious youth, set out to do great things. We plan to cure cancer or travel to Mars. We hope to make a billion dollars or get listed in the Fortune 500. We anticipate political, artistic, or economic success. In the end we experience disappointment or get downright jaded. Why, because we accomplished nothing? No. We just didn't get to check some of the big things off of our to-do list; but this doesn't mean we failed.

A public official may never be elected to the highest office in the land, but he can still work for the highest good of those around him. A physician may not invent the next great vaccine, but she can still care competently and compassionately for the patients that trust her. A stay at home mom may have traded a profitable career for sippy-cups and Pampers, but she will still make a world of difference to the ankle-biters pulling on the hem of her blue jeans. A backwoods pastor may never fill stadiums like Billy Graham, but he can still marry, baptize, guide, and love the modest congregation under his care.

Do these unexceptional things and ordinary people matter? You bet they do; more to God than anyone else. So do what you can. God will take care of the rest.

Ronnie McBrayer

Ode To Barley

I adopted a cat from a shelter once. Once. It was years ago while at one of those big-box pet stores. The local shelter had an entire gaggle of animals up for adoption. A sweet little tuxedo-colored cat named Barley caught my eye and it was love at first sight. At least it was love for me. So I paid my money, bought all the kitty supplies I needed on the spot, and took him home. At the time I was just out of school and living in a basement apartment. I deduced that he would be good company and might even help woo dates back to my bachelor pad.

Upon releasing Barley from his carrier, a terrifying metamorphosis overtook him. The sweet, purring cat of the animal shelter turned into a ferocious, demon-possessed beast that commenced to running laps around my apartment. He clung to my window screens. He swatted and hissed at me. He attempted to climb the walls. He howled and hollered like his tail was on fire. This cat was crack-addict crazy.

After two hours of this I called the shelter. After describing Barley's transformation into Beelzebub I said, "Look, I'm bringing this damn cat back." The shelter was quick to point out that the evening was now very late and I couldn't get my money back. "Keep the money," I said. It was either him or me.

It took a pair of blacksmith gloves and a set of grilling tongs to get him back in the box. And I lost a little skin and blood too, but we were both glad when it was all over.

Sometimes you get what you pay for. Sometimes you get a little more than that. Jesus said it would be like this.

Jesus once said, "The kingdom of God is like a mustard seed." There is the idea in those words that what begins as something small and subtle, explodes into something extraordinary and grand. The meager seed will finally become a full grown. But, as is usual with Jesus' words, there is more here than meets the eye. Mustard was an important herb in biblical days. It was used to flavor food, to treat respiratory troubles, or made into a muscle liniment; an ancient version of Ben Gay.

Mustard could be found growing wild all over Palestine. It was a nuisance. Like crabgrass or kudzu it tended to take over every where it went. Even when it was domesticated and brought into the garden, if not managed carefully, it would break lose and overrun the rest of the crops. The point that Jesus seems to be making is not just that this kingdom of God is something that starts small and ends big. Rather, this kingdom has intrusive, takeover qualities about it. A mustard seed could not leave well enough alone. That is the nature of the kingdom of God and the reign of Christ.

Generally, we want just enough Jesus to bring a little flavor to our life. We'll use him for medicinal purposes to fetch us comfort when we have no other options. We'll bring him home for a little company. But Jesus isn't a pet. He doesn't spring into action like a pill in a bottle or a genie in a lamp. If we think we can invite Christ into our lives and keep him contained, even quarantined, taking only therapeutic doses of him, we've got another thought coming.

Jesus is not here to spice up our life. He has come to take over.

To take Christ into our well-ordered, well-kept lives is in many ways to only ask for trouble, for he will not leave well-enough alone. He will not let us have our own way. He will not be happy until his rule in and over our lives is complete. Our careers, our children, our possessions, our churches, our generosity, our hearts, our minds, our imaginations, our past failures, our futures, our plans, our worries, our ambitions: He wants it all, and will not rest until he has it.

I sometimes fight him. I howl and cry when he invades spaces in my life I do not want to give to him. I swat and hiss. Ultimately, however, he always seems to win. Because it's either him or me. One of us, and only one of us, can be in control.

The Preacher

I grew up with a lot of religious rules. To violate these rules was to subject oneself to the violence of God. You may be familiar with these rules. No drinking, no smoking, no dancing, no mixed-bathing (a prospect that always intrigued my teenage mind), no Sabbath-breaking (though we did not actually gather on the Sabbath), and absolutely no questioning of religious authority.

Religious authority was bound up in "The Preacher." The big Baptist and Methodist churches downtown had a pastor. The Presbyterians had an elder. The one fledgling Catholic parish on the edge of town had a priest. I didn't meet a Jew until high school, so I didn't even know what a rabbi was; but in my little ecclesiastical world, we had The Preacher.

He was the combined concoction of teacher, prophet, taskmaster, guardian, and enforcer. I'm certain he cut his grass in a three piece suit, didn't know a single curse word, and all his children were adopted because to have sex with his wife was certainly too worldly, too carnal to consider.

The world in which The Preacher lived was black and white with no shades of gray, no mystery, no ambiguities. There were only hard and fast rules. You were in or you were out. If you wanted to know which you were, just ask him. He would tell you, and he used the pulpit to do exactly that.

On Sundays he became an inferno of Puritan proportions. Animated, wringing with sweat, almost always discarding his suit coat and loosening his tie, he implored and coerced us sinners down the aisle to the mourner's bench. It usually worked. Someone "repented" most every service, even if it took thirty verses of "Just As I Am" to force the issue. I remember those altar calls as being more than lengthy. They were nerve rattling wars of attrition. Who would win this night: The Preacher or the sinner? Sometimes I felt compelled to go forward just so the whole thing would end.

It was The Preacher who arrived at Henrietta Egleston Children's Hospital on an April Saturday afternoon. My younger brother, Timothy, had been hospitalized since early January with a faulty heart valve and a growing laundry list of complications. He had not yet celebrated his first birthday but already he had had his chest cracked open like a melon, his kidneys had failed, his lungs had collapsed, and a Staph infection in his right elbow had resulted in the amputation of his arm almost at the shoulder to save his life; a life that hung by a thread.

My parents certainly needed emotional and spiritual support, a pastoral presence. The Preacher arrived on cue. But he was anything but comforting. I was at the hospital the day he visited and within ear shot when I heard The Preacher say the most horrible words to my parents. In paraphrase he said, "Surely you have committed some terrible sin for God to visit this kind of judgment on you and your family."

Even as an eight-year-old, I was flabbergasted. Why my parents didn't take this religious charlatan out back to the woodshed I do not know. To this day those words still burn my ears.

Is this the God of Christianity? Is this the kind of God behind our faith? Is this vindictive deity even worthy of our worship? I think not. While this might be the god of The Preacher, it is not the God revealed to us in the person of Jesus the Christ. For in Christ we find truth and grace, not this kind of crass judgmentalism.

Jesus doesn't walk into hospital rooms, his fat belly pushing against the buttons of his tailored pen stripes, handing out indictments of guilt to the innocent. No, this Jesus sits down and weeps with the suffering. He opens his arms to the brutalized and confused. And while he doesn't always, if ever, provide us with the answers we long for, he walks with us in the mystery of life and death.

I never accepted those words spoken in that ICU waiting room. Maybe I've spent the last thirty years trying to disprove them. I hope you won't accept them either.

The love of Christ always trumps the hardness of men's hearts. And for that, I say thanks to be to God.

My Last $5

Most every school day I walk my boys to the bus stop. We talk each morning about the day to come. We double-check homework. We might say a prayer for the day. Sometimes we play with a football or kick the soccer ball as we wait. But you can be certain of one thing every morning, as sure as the sun rising and even more assured than that big yellow bus rounding the corner: Those boys will ask me for money.

Who knew that elementary school could be so expensive? If it's not lunch money they need, then it's money for extra milk, or ice cream, or some over-priced fundraiser, or a book fair, or a snack after school, or for orphans in the Congo. I thought I would get a reprieve from dropping the big money until college; or at least until high school. These boys are nickel-and-diming me to death.

On one recent morning one of my sons was harassing me for five bucks. He wanted to buy some cheesy poster or a bag of pencil erasers or a timeshare in the Caymans. I can't remember which. I opened my wallet and there was a single, crisp five-dollar-bill. It was all the cash I had. So, in a brilliant flash of fatherly wisdom, I decided this was a teachable moment in sacrifice and gratitude. I took out the five-spot and held it before my son.

"This is all the money I have to my name," I pleaded. And in a masterful appeal to the boy's altruistic side I said, "You can have this last five dollars if you really need it. But if you take it, I will have no money for lunch today. I will be hungry until I get home tonight."

The bus pulled up to the stop with flashing lights and an open door. My son looked at me, looked at the bus, snatched the five-dollar-bill and rode away.

I'm not planning on receiving any nursing home visits from him in my golden years.

There is one simple truth about every person: We are selfish. Warlords, successful Fortune 500 CEOs, groveling yes-men and impulsive third-graders all operate with the same premise, the same self-centeredness: To get what they want, damn the consequences to others.

Followers of Jesus are not immune to this. Once, two of Jesus' disciples made an incredibly bigheaded request. "When your kingdom comes," the brothers James and John Zebedee asked Jesus, "May we sit in places of honor, one on your right and the other on your left?"

These men anticipated the day when Jesus would rule the world with all political, economic, religious, and military power at his disposal. He would sit on his throne in the capital city of the world. Where did they see themselves fitting into this mix? At the summit. They wanted to be the VPs and VIPs, the trusted advisors, the seconds in command at the top of the heap. This request threw the entire ensemble of disciples into chaos. The other Jesus-followers lost their cool with the two brothers. But I don't think they were filled with righteous indignation. Hardly.

James and John had simply beat the others to the punch. The group's anger flowed from the fact that James and John might just get what everyone else had been privately wishing for. But the Zebedee request is not a display of instinctive conceit. It is more a demonstration of ignorance; for the kingdom of God does not operate by the rules of this world. The kingdom of God has no place for selfishness, for egoism, and the pandering agendas of the want-to-bes.

Jesus responded to his disciples with these words: "When people get a little power, see how quickly it goes to their heads. But it's not going to be that way with you. Whoever wants to be great must become a servant. Whoever wants to be first among you must become a slave."

A servant? A slave? Wait a second! A servant doesn't have any rights! A slave doesn't get what they want! These are stations in life where one gets abused and mistreated, exploited and ignored!

Exactly. For this is the upside down way in which the kingdom of God breaks free in the world, through the weakness and vulnerability of those who choose to imitate the Christ who gave himself up for others.

Keeping the Faith

Who Will Roll Away The Stone?

My family possesses a noticeable lack of creativity. At least it seems that way. Because every time we gather – for a reunion, a holiday dinner, or what have you – we always tell the same old family stories. I can recite them from memory.

There is the yarn about my granddaddy shooting up White's Pool Hall one night, drunk as a wheelbarrow. Or the time my older relatives nearly dropped my cousin Curt into the chicken pit. And the time my eighty-plus grandmother fearlessly pulled a snake barehanded out of the plumbing of my aunt's house. And then my favorite: Uncle Lamar, the Baptist preacher, couldn't get his tractor started on one particularly cold morning. He cursed and kicked it, losing all resemblance of his religion. He awoke the next morning to find that his tractor had slipped out of gear and rolled down the hill, through the barbed wire fence, and into the catfish pond. His sermon the following Sunday was a beautiful discourse on divine retribution for losing one's temper.

Of course, one of my own experiences has been added to the family litany. And I must endure its retelling at least annually. I've grown so tired of the punch line I can barely retell it here. I was only eight years old and spending a week with an aunt and uncle. Above their little home, resting quietly on the hillside, was a massive rock, pushed there by bulldozers building a new road. This behemoth was the size of a couple of Volkswagen Vanagons.

We were sitting on the front porch and my uncle said casually, "Sure hope that rock never rolls down the hill. Why, it would roll right through the house and kill us all."

I didn't sleep a wink the rest of my stay. I was filled with the blubbering terror that we would all be crushed in our sleep as this malicious rock unhinged itself from its resting place. The headlines the next day would recount the tragic story of a man and woman squashed to death in their bed.

The real heartbreak would be the demise of their innocent nephew who was only visiting for a few days. After two sleepless nights my uncle cut my stay off early and drove me home in a blowing snow storm. It was the only way any of us were going to get any sleep.

Crippling fears. High anxiety. Sleepless nights. Rolling rocks. It sounds a lot like Easter morning. The Gospel tells the old story of a group of women walking to Jesus' tomb early that Sunday morning. These ladies were crushed with grief, sleepless since the crucifixion of their Lord. As their feet shuffle toward the grave side, they have every intention of anointing the hastily buried body of Jesus. There is only one problem: A rock the size of a couple of Volkswagen Vanagons covered the entrance.

They wonder aloud to each other, "How will we get to Jesus' body? How can we pay our respects and embalm him properly?" And then they ask the supreme question of Easter Sunday morning – "Who will roll away the stone?"

Who indeed? The rock, placed over those ancient tombs to keep grave robbers and animals off the corpse, weighed tons. A cohort of soldiers guarding the site only complicated matters further.

We will all ask that question at some point. Who will do for us what we cannot do ourselves? Who is able to do the impossible? Who will roll away the stone? The stone of death. The stone of separation from our loved ones. The stone of fear and dread. The stone of dashed hopes and unfinished lives. The stone of finality that is just too heavy to move.

We know of course that upon their arrival to the tomb, these dear ladies found the stone already rolled away. Jesus had taken up his life again, breaking through the power of death, paving a highway into the kingdom of God. No stone could possibly keep him in the grave. No crucifixion could rob him of life. No Roman governor was powerful enough to keep him held down. No amount of injustice would be allowed to prevail over this perfectly lived life.

Who will roll away the stone? Jesus already has. Now that's a family story worth repeating.

Blue Bomber

I love it when I get the chance to take my children to school. It doesn't happen often, so if I can take them, I do. Why? Because I know there will come a day when they will be far too cool to be seen with their father. Soon enough, being driven to school in a Subaru by their old man just won't be hip enough.

When my own father used to take me to school it was great. I didn't care about the type of car he drove or its color or what others thought of me or anything like that. I was proud enough just to be seen with him rather than getting off the bus with everyone else. Of course that changed as I got older.

When I was in high school my father drove an aged blue Chevrolet station wagon my sister and I not-so-affectionately called the "Blue Bomber." I say it was "blue" but that is not completely accurate. This old ride was about fifteen years past its prime. So it was more rust-colored than blue, the paint having faded to oxidation a decade earlier. Worse, it had a hole in the muffler large enough to stuff a watermelon. This resulted in a symphony of strange, loud, guttural noises. And to add insult to injury, the windshield wipers stopped working some time before I hit puberty. On rainy and frosty days my dad would have to drive with his head craned out the window to see the road.

So it's not hard to imagine that my begging would begin every morning on the way to school: "Dad, please drop me off at the driveway or at the far end of the parking lot," I would desperately implore. Because the last thing I wanted was to be seen in this image-killer. Rain, sleet, snow, dead of night – these never troubled me. I was happy to walk through hell itself if it meant putting some distance between me and the Blue Bomber.

Sadly, my father never listened. Undeterred he would drive that rolling junkyard right up to the front door of Gordon Central High School and force me out. In front of the jocks; the hottest girls of the Junior and Senior class; and the kids too chic to be caught in a deteriorating station wagon.

Maybe he enjoyed destroying my high school reputation. It sure seemed that way. After I slinked out of the backseat each morning he would stomp the gas, belching black smoke and sulfur all over me. With his head cocked out the window, he backfired and rattled over the horizon, smiling all the way.

My Father's mode of transportation still bothers me. No, I'm not speaking of dad's station wagon. That old thing went to the graveyard the year I left for college (How's that for timing?). I'm speaking of our Father who is in heaven. For reasons I am always at a loss to explain, God has chosen to communicate his good news for the world through this bewildering vehicle called the church. Still, he seems very determined that the church, belching, knocking and smoking as it goes, deliver his grace to others. And this embarrasses me.

I'm embarrassed by the filthy extravagance the church spends upon itself. I'm embarrassed by the flashy televangelists who shuck and jive more like hucksters than rough-and-tumble tellers of the truth. I'm embarrassed by the harsh gracelessness exhibited by card-carrying Christians. But that's not the end of it. I'm embarrassed by myself; by my own failures and hypocrisy, the way my profession as a follower of Christ so rarely matches my actions.

I wonder why God puts up with us all. He is the one who should be embarrassed. Yet, he is not. He just keeps guiding this old, antiquated vehicle on its way. Seemingly past its prime, the church tumbles down the road, barely holding speed, God smiling all the time.

I'm no Pollyanna thinking the church is a faultless hotrod, burning up the streets. Na, it's a clunker. But it is still the vehicle God has chosen. Maybe we should be less concerned with what people think, and do our best to enjoy the ride.

God Is In The Goulash

"Do you believe that God is in total control of this world?" Someone asked me that question the other day.

We had been discussing the difficulties of life and the trajectory our planet so dishearteningly seems to be headed. Being asked about God's control of the universe is a lot like being asked, "Have you stopped beating your wife?" Either answer you give condemns you. So rather than answering "yes" or "no," I opted to talk about my Aunt Betty's goulash.

Goulash is supposed to be an Eastern European stew of sorts. For my Aunt Betty I think it is more a way of cleaning out the refrigerator. She puts meat in it; noodles, tomatoes, paprika, onions, coffee grounds, peanut butter, grass clippings from the last time Uncle Joe emptied the bagger on the lawn mower. Everything. It consists of all these strange, typically unrelated ingredients. But my Aunt Betty is a good cook. Her dish tastes pretty darn good in the end. In the hands of a lesser cook, however, I'm sure goulash would be a culinary disaster.

This is my chosen metaphor to explain God's "control" over the world. God takes all the ingredients of life as they jumble together in the pot: Heartaches, triumphs, failures, and accomplishments; bad decisions, injustices, and hope; our creativity and our stupidity – all these things. We can't imagine how any of this fits together.

How can this be worth anything? Yet, God is able to make something wonderful out of it.

He masterfully brews this magnificent gumbo we call life, and it will taste pretty darn good in the end. But don't dip in your spoon and taste it too early. It's not done yet. It still has a ways to go. God is still bringing it all to a boil, waiting for a few essential ingredients to be added to the mix before it's put on the table.

This then, is the Christian hope: God is redeeming the world through his Son, Jesus the Christ. We believe God is putting his creation to rights and will accomplish this purpose no matter how gloomy life sometimes appears.

So, does God control this world? Sure he does, just not in the mechanical, unconscious way we may have always imagined. I don't think he is pulling levers and punching buttons dictating the minutia of life. He seems to have left a great deal of autonomy for us his creations. In the greatest act of grace short of the cross itself, God has given us a role to play in the redemption of creation. His good pleasure is, amazingly, to do his will and work through us. That God is all-powerful over his world, masterfully cooking in his kitchen, does not diminish, negate, or marginalize our role and responsibility in the least. God will do what God will do. You and I must do the same.

Now, if I was God, and you should thank God I'm not, I would have never entrusted my good creation to beings so irresponsible, so short-sighted, so corrupt and depraved. Yet, this is exactly what

God has done. We haven't earned this glorious responsibility. We don't deserve it, but it is ours. What will we do with it…What will you do with it?

Frodo, in J.R.R. Tolkien's classic "Lord of the Rings" series is that little hobbit on whom the One Ring falls. He and only he must bear this terrible possession to the fires of Mount Doom to save Middle Earth. He protests his assignment, having not asked for this awful burden that has fallen into his hands. He says to his mentor and guide, Gandalf, "I wish the ring had never come to me. I wish none of this had happened."

And how we wish our world was different, just like young Frodo.

But Gandalf wisely responds, "So do all who see such times. But that is not for us to decide. All we have to decide is what to do with the time that we are given."

If given an audience with God we might be so bold as to ask him, "Why don't you do something about starving children, genocide, the violation of the innocent, and unending war? Why don't you intervene in your world?"

Such queries are dangerous. Not because God can't handle it; he certainly can. But he just might ask us the same questions.

About The Author

Ronnie McBrayer was born in the foothills of the North Georgia Appalachians. He barely – just barely – survived the fire-and-brimstone, fundamentalist, dispensational, hyper-legalistic, KJV-only, rabid-God indoctrination of his hard shell Baptist-reared childhood.

But in the great comedy of God, Ronnie has spent his adulthood in ministry, both preaching in and protesting against; both loving and loathing; both running away from and returning to the church. The faith he is trying to keep isn't in organized religion, however, God knows. It is in Jesus.

Ronnie has been a pastor, chaplain, leader in social justice ministries, a musician, and a writer. But the role he enjoys most is being husband to Cindy and father to Blayze, Bryce, and Braden.

He holds degrees in Christian Education and Theology, with post-graduate studies in Bio-Ethics and Critical Incident Stress Management (The latter were courses necessary to aid himself and others to survive the church, you know).

He is a dynamic and compassionate speaker, the author of several books including *But God Meant It for Good* (Smyth and Helwys), and he can be found every Monday morning at his desk pounding out another article for his weekly newspaper column, "Keeping the Faith."

Ronnie McBrayer

For additional author information or to secure syndication of "Keeping the Faith" in your local newspaper or publication, visit Ronnie's website at www.leavingsalem.net.